YEARNING
to know
GOD'S WILL

YEARNING
to *know*
GOD'S WILL

◆

A Workbook for
Discerning
God's Guidance
for Your Life

D A N N Y E. M O R R I S

ZondervanPublishingHouse
Academic and Professional Books
Grand Rapids, Michigan

A Division of HarperCollinsPublishers

Yearning To Know God's Will
Copyright © 1991 by Danny E. Morris

Requests for information should be addressed to:
Zondervan Publishing House
Academic and Professional Books
1415 Lake Drive S.E.
Grand Rapids, Michigan 49506

Library of Congress Cataloging-in-Publication Data

Morris, Danny E.
    Yearning to know God's will : discernment principles that help you know the
will of God / Danny E. Morris.
        p.   cm.
    ISBN 0-310-75491-7
    1. Discernment of spirits. 2. God–Will. I. Title.
    BV5083.M67 1991
    248.4–dc20   91-17742
                                                                                    CIP

Unless otherwise noted, all Scripture quotations are from the Revised Standard
Version of the Bible, Copyright 1946, 1952, 1971, 1973 by the Division of Christian
Education, National Council of Churches of Christ in the United States of America,
and used by permission.

Edited by Cindy Lanning
Interior design by Louise Bauer
Cover design by David Marty Design
Cover photo by Chad Ehlers, 1989

Printed in the United States of America

91 92 93 94 95 96 / AM / 10 9 8 7 6 5 4 3 2 1

To
Rosalie
who freely shares her gift
and makes it a gift to me
by often standing
in light
that I cannot see

Contents

SECTION THREE
A Retreat Format

In Appreciation

I want to express my appreciation to the following persons and groups who helped and encouraged me in the completion of this book:

Hugh and Fran Lake (Englewood); Dorothy and Douglas Steere; Fr. Timothy Kelly, OSB; W. G. Henry; Claude Whitehead; Parker Palmer; Don Saliers; Maxie Dunnam; Ross Whetstone; James K. Wagner; Robert Mulholland; Sr. Rita Anne Houlihan, r.c.; Byron Jones; Stephen Bryant; Paul Jones; Fr. Ed Farrell; Steve Harper; Alan Morris; and the five groups at River Road United Methodist Church, Richmond, Virginia; and the three groups at St. Paul's United Methodist Church, Mt. Juliet, Tennessee.

Introduction

1. Spiritual discernment is one of the gifts of the Spirit that St. Paul mentions in 1 Corinthians 12:4–11. He begins the discussion by explaining:

> Now there are varieties of gifts but the same Spirit; and
> there are varieties of service, but the same Lord; and
> there are varieties of workings, but it is the same God
> who inspires them all in every one. To each is given
> the manifestation of the Spirit for the common good.
>
> *Vv. 4–7*

In verse 10, one of the gifts Paul describes is "the ability to distinguish between spirits." This is the gift of spiritual discernment.

2. Spiritual discernment has always come hard for me, so hard that I once concluded that I could not do it. After all, discernment is a spiritual *gift*—and I obviously had not been given that gift. I felt I could do nothing but shrug and trudge on. And trudge I did for long periods of my life. In one instance I spent almost a year trying to discern God's will on an important matter that would affect the rest of my life. During that year I felt the intense frustration of being dragged across the cutting edge of indecision. That was a long time to be in turmoil. It was tough. My only saving grace was that I would not commit to a decision until I felt that I had clear knowledge of God's will. I now realize that my reluctance to act was an important part of the discerning process instead of an absence of discernment at work in me. But not knowing that at the time made it a year of anguish.

3. Because of my experience with spiritual discernment—or seeming lack of it—this has been a compelling subject for me for a number of years. I have concluded that discernment is a gift the Holy Spirit gives to persons seeking for special wisdom. All of us are called to cultivate, nurture, and increase our capacities to discern God's will.

4. God wants *everyone* to know God's will. God doesn't

withhold grace, play games, or tease us to test our faithfulness or our worthiness to be trusted with divine insight. I am convinced that God is far more prone to human revelation than I am to divine encounter. God's will is that you and I, everyone, and our faith communities should discern and act upon God's will.

5. The eight narratives tell of relationships that illustrate, rather than define, discernment. Discernment is not an academic discipline to be studied, analyzed, and defined so that it can be understood. It is to be experienced for itself—then understanding will come.

6. At the end of Narrative One we consider a simple definition, but that, or any other definition of discernment, will not convince any one of us to become a discerning person. We love God and want to do God's will. That is the reason we strive to discern it!

7. Since the narratives illustrate rather than define discernment, you will not "understand" discernment just by reading the narratives, any more than the disciples understood Jesus simply by talking to him. Rather, they related to him by walking with him, living with him, and loving him. In the same way, we shall come to understand discernment by experiencing it and remembering what Jesus said to do—and then doing it! (After all, the value of discernment is not in just knowing God's will but in doing it.) This workbook will give you a way to do that.

8. My interest in discernment influences the way I read Scripture, for I notice how it is filled with examples of discernment. Some are highly dramatic while others describe discernment in everyday encounters. The Old and New Testaments contain live-action stories of real people loving God and, therefore, discerning God's will for the community or for themselves.

9. When I read the Bible, I am almost overwhelmed with the blessed ones, the "smart cookies," who practiced discernment as a way of life. Because we in our day still long to understand and practice it, let's call to mind a few whose lives teach us about discernment.

10. Elijah was a first-class discerner:

> "Go forth and stand upon the mount before
>   the Lord." And behold, the Lord passed by, and
> a great and strong wind rent the mountains,
>   and broke into pieces the rocks before the Lord,
> but the Lord was not in the wind; and after the
>   wind an earthquake, but the Lord was not in the
> earthquake; and after the earthquake a fire; but the
>   Lord was not in the fire; and after the fire a

still small voice. [One version says, "the soft
    whisper of a voice."]
And when Elijah heard it, he wrapped his face
    in his mantle and went out and stood at the entrance
of the cave.

1 Kings 19:11–13

11. That day on the mountain, Elijah experienced a demonstration of God's pyrotechnics. He looked at many things and had probably looked in many places as he tried to find God. But Elijah came to *see* that God was nowhere that he had looked. Instead, Elijah found God "in the still small voice" deep within—in the "soft whisper of a voice." *Hearing*, like *seeing*, is a means of discernment.

12. And, of course, we think of Samuel. Samuel was trying to pick a new king to be the anointed one of Israel. He auditioned the first of Jesse's sons. Because Eliab was tall and good looking, Samuel immediately thought he was the one. But the Lord gave Samuel a short course in discernment as he prepared to evaluate his next contestant.

   . . . the Lord said to Samuel, "Do not
    look on his appearance or on the height
of his stature, because I have rejected him;
    for the Lord sees not as man sees;
man looks on the outward appearance,
    but the Lord looks on the heart."

1 Sam. 16:7

13. Samuel inspected one after another of Jesse's sons until seven had been rejected. Samuel asked whether these were all he had. One more son, the youngest of the brothers, was watching sheep. Samuel told Jesse to send for him; that he was not leaving until he came.

   . . . he sent, and brought him in. Now he was ruddy
    and had beautiful eyes, and was handsome.
And the Lord said, "Arise, anoint him; for this is he."
    Then Samuel took the horn of oil, and anointed him
in the midst of his brothers; and the spirit of the
    Lord came mightly upon David
from that day forward.

1 Sam. 16:12–13

Samuel's experience teaches us that spiritual discernment is the capacity to *see* as God sees.

14. I think also of Moses, whom God called to liberate his people from Egypt. Moses immediately demurred, ". . . but I am slow of speech and of tongue" (Ex. 4:10b). But Moses continued to communicate with God to discern the truth of the call he was hearing and the gifts God would provide. And God provided. Aaron spoke for Moses, and Moses had regular conversations with God. Day by day, in the little things and the big things, Moses listened and discerned God's will for God's people.

15. Let's not forget Solomon who prayed for an *understanding mind (heart)*: ". . . to govern thy people, that I may discern between good and evil; for who is able to govern this thy great people?" (1 Kings 3:9).

16. Jacob was so human, so real, a great model of discernment for us because he had trouble discerning. He had tricked his brother, Esau, and his father, Isaac, causing a deep rift in his family. After twenty years in exile from his family, Jacob split with his father-in-law, Laban, and took his wives, Rachel and Leah, and their children and herds and headed back to Palestine and his previous home. But, first, he had to face Esau, whom Jacob had tricked him out of their father's blessing. The brothers would soon meet again, and they needed, and wanted, to keep from killing each other. But a deeper issue faced Jacob: he cared about the Promise. Whether he was to go back or go forward, he was trying to find God.

17. That night when he is alone, he wrestles with a man who cannot prevail against him, for Jacob is very strong. God wants him to fulfill the Promise. He will not give up the Promise. In the process, he has to be humbled and he also has to prevail to prove his mettle. Finally, the man says, "Let me go, for the day is breaking." But Jacob will not let the man go until he receives a blessing. Then Jacob, who had been wrestling with the man all night, said something like, "By the way, who are you anyway?" Now, there is a slow discerner!

18. "Why is it that you ask my name?" the man replies. And there he blesses him.

19. When it was all over the next morning, Jacob was not the same. He not only had a blessing, he had a new name—Israel, ". . . for you have striven with God and with men, and have prevailed," the unidentified man explained. And he had a lifetime limp because of the fierce wrestling.

20. Discernment had come to Jacob. "Jacob called the name of the place Peniel, saying, "For I have seen God face to face and yet my life is preserved" (Gen. 32:22–32). The next day, after making peace with Esau, Jacob went to the city of Shechem in the land of

Canaan, and from there to Bethel. At Bethel, God appeared to Jacob again, "And God said to him, 'I am God Almighty: be fruitful and multiply; a nation and a company of nations shall come from you, and kings shall spring from you. The land which I gave to Abraham and Isaac I will give to you, and I will give the land to your descendants, after you'" (Gen. 35:11–12). The Promise! The Promise!

21. Mary, the mother of Jesus, knew the struggles and benefits of discerning God's will. What the angel told Mary was as hard for her to understand as to believe. "But Mary kept all these things, pondering [discerning] them in her heart" (Luke 1:19). Perhaps one of the first discernment questions for Mary was, "Is Jesus really who the angel said he would be?"

22. The wisemen and the shepherds confirmed what the angel said. There was no question for Elizabeth, Zechariah, Simeon, and Anna the prophetess. The star also seemed to agree as it poured its eternal brilliance over Bethlehem for the first time. Mary had much to ponder in Simeon's statement:

> "Behold, this child is set for the fall and rising again of many in
> Israel,
>   and for a sign that is spoken against;
> (and a sword will pierce through your own soul also),
>   that the thoughts out of many hearts may be revealed."
> *Luke 2:34–35*

Mary must have wondered what that meant. Day after day, in little and big ways, Mary longed to know and understand—to discern—the meaning of Simeon's prophetic words.

23. Here is a lesson for us: When we long to know and do God's will—day by day as Mary did—it is natural to turn to God in special times, when we need special wisdom, as Mary did.

24. Let's not forget Joseph. His situation was very perplexing. His fiancée was pregnant, and he had nothing to do with it. She became pregnant in a miraculous way—by the Holy Spirit. Joseph struggled with whether to divorce her or to stay with her. At first, he "resolved to divorce her quietly" (Matt. 1:19). But then God's will became clear for him—that he take her for his wife.

25. The brilliant, winsome Stephen found a deeper wisdom than the crowd possessed that put him to death. As they stoned him, he prayed, "Lord, do not hold this sin against them" (Acts 7:60). God gave him a profound capacity to see a reality that the crowd could not see; he knew a relationship they did not know.

26. We see discernment in full operation in the early church in their way of being together and making decisions. Dissension broke out over whether gentile Christians had to be circumcised in keeping with Jewish law. Paul and Barnabas went to Jerusalem when this issue became a major problem. Peter spoke eloquently about the place of circumcision: "We believe that we shall be saved through the grace of the Lord Jesus, just as they will" (Acts 15:11). Paul and Barnabas, and others, spoke. James sided with Peter. These men were not trying to resolve the issue in an ordinary way; knowing God's will was their goal and spiritual discernment was operative among them. We begin to notice the language of discernment: "It seemed good to the apostles and the elders . . ." (v. 22).

27. When this story began in Acts 15, the church was already polarized. If they had argued and chosen sides to settle the issue, it would have taken only the arrival of Paul and Barnabas to accelerate a split in the church. But they chose a higher way. In fact, discernment must have been their normal way to be together, for the Bible does not say they chose the way of discernment. They did it as though they had been doing it all along. They could experience discernment because they were experienced in discernment. The happy and right result was that God's will on a thorny issue was clearly discerned.

28. That is spiritual discernment at work within the Body of Christ. The ancient model of the church is to make decisions under the guidance of the Holy Spirit and in the spirit of unity.

29. The way of discernment is intended to be our higher way to be the church, but we often settle for a lower way—the adversarial approach to make decisions by choosing up sides and taking a vote. We spend our time and energy arguing and defending various points of view, instead of using our energy to *listen* to know God's heart, God's mind, God's plan. The spiritual-discernment style of being together and making hard decisions is revolutionary, but it was practiced at "First Church," Jerusalem, and it is commended to our churches today.

How To Use This Resource

We can all increase our capacity to love God and to discern his will if we study and practice the principles of discernment set forth in this book, which has three parts. Section One is five narratives on personal discernment and the workbook content for five weeks, followed by the format for five weekly meetings. Section Two has three narratives on corporate discernment, followed by workbook content for three weeks and the format for three weekly meetings. Section Three is a retreat model for the group that chooses to implement principles of discernment within the congregation.

Some years ago when Maxie Dunnam first discussed his goal of preparing a workbook to help people learn how to pray, I questioned whether prayer could be learned through a workbook. He, however, was convinced of its possibility. As we rode together to work each day, we worked on his latest material. He kept grinding away at writing, we kept working on content, and I kept telling him that *I didn't think we were supposed to be able to do this*. Now that he has written six workbooks, I know I was wrong. The workbook format helps people experientially appropriate for their life situations content that is biblical, theological, and spiritual. Such workbooks are a breakthrough in formulating personal and corporate learning resources.

THE WORKBOOK PLAN

Each of the eight units in the workbook section encompasses a week for the participant. Each unit's content is divided into seven daily portions. Thirty minutes each day will be enough time to cover the material. Most persons find greater consistency when they do it at about the same time each day—preferably the first thing in the morning.

Sunday is a special day, Day 7 in the workbook. Day 7 is always devoted to your spiritual discernment within the congregation. Study your workbook before you go to church. It will call you to be a spiritual presence within the congregation, instead of being only an observer in worship.

PERSONAL AND CORPORATE DISCERNMENT

Most books I have read on spiritual discernment say much about personal discernment and little about corporate discernment. That may be because corporate discernment is more difficult to experience. But corporate discernment is essential to our living the fullness of the Christian faith and strengthening the body of Christ.

You can utilize this text on three levels: (1) Read the narratives in preparation for doing the workbook. You will notice that narrative paragraphs are numbered in bold type. In the daily lessons are references to paragraph and page numbers for easier access to the material you are to reread. (2) Use the workbook, which incorporates the narratives, and *meet with a small group to experience the corporate nature of spiritual discernment.* (3) Participate in the retreat format with others in your church who have completed the first two levels. The retreat format provides a beginning corporate effort to introduce these discernment principles into the life of your congregation. The greatest value of the book is here.

You will find that the small group provides a model of the body of Christ, for which there is no substitute for spiritual discernment. It is the essential testing ground for the process and results of spiritual discernment. What is discerned to be the will of God must be offered to the body of Christ to be prayed about, tested, and affirmed or corrected. If confirmation is not possible within the body, then discernment is not complete.

Everyone who is serious about discerning God's will is eager to test that understanding within the church. The small-group setting provides a working model of this ministry. The retreat is also valuable for introducing these principles to the leaders who can make a difference in the future of the church.

GUIDELINES FOR THE GROUP

- Eight to twelve persons is an ideal group size.
- It is recommended that one person lead the entire study.
- A group meeting of one and a half hours is ample time.
- Each participant needs a workbook.
- Meet for getting acquainted and orientation prior to beginning the eight weeks in the workbook.
- Have a group meeting at or near the end of each of the eight weeks, preferably on Sunday evening.

THE LEADER:

- Is responsible for securing and distributing necessary materials and for arranging for a suitable meeting place—preferably at the church. (If meeting in a home, arrange for a minimum of interruptions from children, pets, phone, etc. If refreshments are served, hold them until the meeting ends.)
- Is responsible for convening the group and coordinating the procedure.
- Will endeavor to keep the group oriented to the time frame

for the session while remaining sensitive to the group's alternating needs for involvement, worship, laughter, quietness, discussion, and celebration.

To foster a sense of togetherness in the group, the intended style of leadership is for the leader to begin with the group-guidance material and read until a specific action is suggested to the group. After the group responds, the leader may proceed by reading aloud the successive points of procedural guidance.

Before the first meeting, have a get-acquainted and orientation meeting (see pages 18–20) so that the group clearly understands the purpose of the group and how it will proceed.

All participants should make a commitment to attend the orientation meeting and all eight small-group sessions, and to be faithful in the workbook process and in punctuality.

D.E.M.
Nashville, Tennessee

Format For Initial Get-Acquainted and Orientation Meeting

- Have participants introduce themselves and tell something about themselves that will interest the others.
- Distribute the workbooks and briefly describe how to use them:
  - Follow the daily workbook format.
  - Allow thirty minutes a day.
  - Attend eight regular group meetings of an hour and a half a week.
  - Be punctual and faithful in attendance at these meetings.
- During this orientation meeting demonstrate the personal, daily format of the workbook as follows:

Two basic movements are to be followed each day in the workbook section: READING and REFLECTION AND RESPONSE. The workbook section will guide you in reading all the narratives, so there is no need to read ahead. Let's work through a couple of typical exercises during this group meeting.

Exercise One: Spiritual Discernment Is for Everyone

READING

- Ask everyone to read the Introduction that begins on page 9. (Omit this if the workbooks were distributed prior to the meeting and participants have already read it.)
- Ask everyone to review the first four paragraphs of the Introduction.

REFLECTION AND RESPONSE (As a group exercise)

Perhaps none of us would be here if spiritual discernment came easily for us!

Think of a particular instance when your discernment of God's will was a long time in coming, or has not come at all. Write it here:

_____

_____

In light of this recollection, have someone read aloud the first four paragraphs of the Introduction. As this is read, any insights that come to you about your situation write here:

_____

_____

_____

_____

The basic premise of this workbook is expressed in the words of the fourth paragraph:

> I have concluded that [spiritual discernment] is a gift the Holy Spirit gives to persons seeking for a special wisdom. But I also believe that all of us are called to cultivate, nurture, and increase our capacities to discern God's will.

Whether you have found spiritual discernment hard or easy, remember that spiritual discernment is for *everyone*.

Exercise Two

Ask each person to select the individual in the Bible (including but not limited to those mentioned in the Introduction) with whom he or she identifies and from whom he or she has learned the most about discernment.

Exercise Three: Making Discernment Personal

Think about three specific areas of your life in which you need to know God's will, and write them here:

_____

_____

_____

Pray about one of these specific needs during a time of silence now. Put a check mark by the one you have selected to pray about. For the time of silence, get comfortable and relax. We will have about three minutes of silence. I will call us out of the silence.

After the silence the leader will share his or her own experience of silence and end by reading the following:

ABOUT SILENCE

Discernment is about *seeing*.

Silence is about *hearing*.

Seeing and hearing are so intermingled in generative power that they are seldom neatly separated. If discernment is our goal, silence will be our practice. Begin with "comfortable silence" and gently lengthen your periods of silence and their frequency until you are having regular meaningful periods of "waiting before the Lord." Begin with where you are comfortable and you will likely find that the gift of silence will grow along with your desire for it.

Describe the workbook process: Allow about a half hour each day to follow the guidance of the workbook.

• Read the narratives as they are indicated.

• Make these weeks a spiritual journey.

• Be prepared and present for the weekly group meetings.

Invite participants to share their feelings or expectations as they begin this study.

Close with a brief audible prayer by the leader.

Personal Discernment

What Is Spiritual Discernment?

> Lord, you heard, and were gracious to me;
>> O Lord, you were my helper
> You turned my grief into dancing,
>> Stripped me of sorrow and clothed me with joy.
> So my heart will sing to you; not weep;
>> Lord, my God, I will praise you forever.
>
> *Psalm 30:10–12*

1. In the critical moments of our lives we find passages of Scripture that speak especially to us. This passage began to hold special meaning to me because of what happened on the way home one day. I have thought since that event that my name should have been written in the margin of Psalm 30.

2. It began on a quiet Saturday afternoon as I returned home from getting a haircut. The rain had ended but the roads were still wet. When I awoke in the hospital five hours later the last thing I remembered was how brightly the sun was reflected off a yellow house directly ahead of me in the little curve of the road. The color was brilliant.

3. I awakened in the midst of family laughter. It was nervous laughter, the kind that revealed my family's relief to see that I had come back to my senses and that I knew where I was again.

4. My daughter said, "In the last four or five hours you have asked about Ruggy (our family dog) over and over again. Ruggy is home and fine. Ruggy didn't get his hair cut today. He was not with you in the car. He is home and fine."

"What happened?"

"Dad . . . you had a head-on collision!"

"Is the car OK? We haven't had it a month."

5. My wife, Rosalie, said, "Yes, the car is fine. It saved your life. Darling, don't worry about the car. We can always get another car. It was a wonderful car because it saved your life."

6. Later I learned how true that was. The other car had skidded slightly going around a tight curve. The driver tried to correct but hit

me head-on about halfway over the line. Then the rear end of that car hit the back of mine, catapulting my car off a twenty-five-foot cliff, through a four-strand barbed wire fence. My car stopped in a cow pasture seventy-five feet from the road. It was bent in the middle, top and bottom, and the steering wheel and steering column were laid flat against the left front door.

7. After three days of care in the hospital and three weeks of recuperation at home, I returned to work. All seemed well again. When I went for a follow-up visit to the neurosurgeon who had attended me in the hospital, I was not prepared for the news he had for me. It is an understatement to say that he was a person of few words: "You look much better than your X-rays. Come back in a month and we will talk about doing a brain shunt."

8. I was devastated. I could not reply. I could not ask questions. I felt he had hit me in the stomach with a brickbat. I walked out of his office like a Zombie. Four C.T. scans and a year later, the prognosis was confirmed by another neurosurgeon: "There is a 50–50 chance you will have to have brain surgery."

9. A 50–50 chance! That was hard to comprehend—especially since there were no discernible signs of a problem except from the X-rays. It was a long, hard journey for me from that first brickbat in the stomach to these words of Scripture that became special for me: "We rejoice in our suffering, knowing that suffering produces endurance, endurance produces character, character produces hope" (Romans 5:4).

10. For a long time I was short on hope as well as on endurance and character. One Saturday morning about a year after the accident, while Rosalie was on duty at the hospital and I was alone in the house, it all tumbled in on me. I stood in front of the bathroom mirror and wept because of the heaviness of this bad dream from which there seemed to be no waking. Throughout the year it had been difficult to pray about all this, except to thank God for an abundance of providential care through the accident. When I hit bottom on that desolate Saturday morning, I could not pray.

11. I could not know on that grim day that I would soon have a kind of workaday, commonplace, on-the-run, unexpected experience of spiritual discernment. That experience also caught me when I was not looking.

12. Friends and I were making plans for a Friday-night outdoor picnic for about sixty people. On Tuesday and Wednesday the weather forecast predicted a thirty-percent chance of rain for Friday night. The less desirable alternative to the picnic would require

totally different planning and a lot of extra effort. By Thursday forecasters predicted a fifty-percent chance of rain. Anxiously we waited it out while putting final touches on alternate plans.

13. It was a beautiful Friday afternoon and evening. The weather could not have been better for our picnic. Then suddenly it came to me! There had been a 50–50 chance of rain and for two days, and we had counted on its raining. We had planned for rain—but all the while there was a fifty-percent chance it *wouldn't* rain. We had counted on the wrong fifty percent!

14. That's it! I had been devastated by my condition because I had counted on, expected, and feared that the wrong fifty percent would prevail. According to the doctors, the possibility that I would not need surgery was as great as that I would. I had thought only about the wrong fifty.

15. Earlier that day I had read Mark 11:24: "Pray about everything and believe and it is yours." I wrote my new breakthrough discovery in my journal: "Prayer and belief are inseparable. My 50-50 chance of needing surgery is an example. If I pray and 'believe' in the negative 50, it will adversely affect my prayer and healing. Healing is enhanced as I pray and believe in the positive 50." Then I put a star by this: "Today's insight is an integrating concept for my life."

16. Prayer *and* belief go hand in hand. Here was more than just a thought or an idea. Here was my discernment of a fundamental truth for my life. It was a truth I had needed desperately. There was nothing mystical or otherworldly about this great discovery.

17. Spiritual discernment comes in the midst of everyday circumstances, for discernment is about seeing—a deeper way of seeing. Rather than issuing from an ecstatic, supertranscendent realm that is foreign to us and would probably frighten people like us, valid and vital spiritual discernment is woven among the common threads of everyday activities. I have had many such experiences and you probably have, too. This encourages me because if my discernings of the Spirit are connected to superreligious experiences or those that transcend religious experiences (such as "out-of-the-body" experiences that characterize New Age thinking), I would tend to be left out.

18. This seeing of a deeper, fundamental truth about myself has helped me see other people more realistically. Many people I know are 50–50 people. It is not uncommon for people to live with broken dreams, health problems, missed opportunities, broken relationships, deep hurts. The losses tend to loom larger than life. If you are a 50–50 person—if you have a 50–50 chance—it matters whether you count on the *better 50* or the *worse 50*. I can tell you that it makes all the difference in the world!

19. I met a young man in Oregon who verified this important discovery. He had lost the sight of one eye and was having great difficulty in handling his loss. After I talked about the importance of believing in the better 50, Byron said, "You are right. I have been devastated, too, because of the loss of my eye. As you were talking, I realized that I still have one good eye. That is my better 50 and I haven't thought anything about it before. I have been thinking only about my loss. What you said was a healing experience for me. I am going to celebrate my better 50."

20. And I have also seen things differently since I have been looking at the better 50. I can pray about my situation now and I couldn't before. The reason I couldn't pray was because I was obsessed with the wrong 50. My prayer and my belief were incongruent. I was trying to pray positively while thinking and believing negatively. Now I focus on the better 50 and pray for it. There is congruence between my praying and believing and hope is built.

21. I am not kidding myself. The other shoe may fall some day. But I am no longer *counting on it*! There is a 50–50 chance that it won't. That is what I am counting on. That makes a dramatic difference in my attitude, my prayer, and my sense of hope.

22. When the neurosurgeon first mentioned the brain shunt, he gave me a brochure describing the apparatus. I was so devastated that I could not look at it. All my energy was sapped by the negative 50. I had none left for looking at the hard facts. Praying for and expecting the better 50 enabled me to think about the surgery, to inquire about the procedure, and to evaluate the risks. What a difference occurred when I began to think that way.

23. Father Edward Farrell is absolutely right when he says, "Discernment is allowing Jesus to pour his Spirit into us, which allows us to recognize the gifts that we have already received."

24. See if you can visualize me standing in front of my bathroom mirror, broken and weeping. Contrast that image with a vision of me expressing to God "my" Scripture from Psalm 30:

> Lord, you heard, and were gracious to me;
> O Lord, you were my helper.
> You turned my grief into dancing.
> Stripped me of sorrow and clothed me with joy.

So my heart will sing to you; not weep;
Lord, my God, I will praise you forever.

25. You can see that I experienced a dramatic shift between those two positions within just a few days. So dramatic and so profound, in fact, that I experienced a life-changing moment of spiritual discernment. I am not the same person now.

* * *

26. I began with the question: What is spiritual discernment? My experience suggests that it is not something that is strange or odd or esoteric or mysterious. It is not a static quality of character but is a gift of God through faith. Spiritual discernment is a capacity to see our lives clearly in the light of God's will. This capacity is potentially available to all of us so that we may live our lives fully in the grace and truth of Jesus Christ.

27. As I began the definition above, I deliberately used the words "my experience suggests" because spiritual discernment is always experiential. Moreover, it ideally happens within the total movement of one's life rather than in isolated events. Spiritual discernment involves a personal and dynamic encounter with God not only in particular situations but in *all* situations. It is ongoing within the human spirit, not a now-and-then spiritual exercise. And, as it was for me, discernment is often the catalyst for new or changed directions or attitudes.

28. Innumerable modes of discernment can work within each of us. Some of the better defined and highly refined are: prayer in all its forms—and intercession in particular; reading and studying Scripture; and all forms of Christian worship. Other means of discernment include meaningful conversation; reading the newspaper or serious, spiritual reading; pondering; any form of deliberate silence; recapitulation, reassessment, and other forms of "taking-the-long-look"; and, of course, the teachings of the church. This list can go on and on to suggest ways that we come to know God.

29. But let us be clear: It is God who changes us. These modes or processes are catalysts or vehicles. We do not glorify spiritual discernment as a method. We use it as a means of glorifying God by our choice to love God and to enter into the dynamic relationship God offers us.

30. Let's look inside the above definition of spiritual discernment. "Spiritual discernment is a capacity to *see*." This connotes a special kind of *seeing*, deep *seeing*, a deep and profound *knowing*. How else can God be truly known? The *seeing* of discernment is more than visual sight. "See" in this context is a packed word, a pregnant symbol that must be freely interchanged with many other words in order to express the variety of ways that we come to *know*, to *hear*, to *understand*, to *respond to*, and to *love* God. All such words suggest that a definite clarity of perception is possible concerning life's deepest matters.

31. Spiritual discernment is a gift of the Holy Spirit, which is mentioned by the apostle Paul in 1 Corinthians 12:4–11. In verse 7, he writes, "To each is given the manifestation of the Spirit for the common good." The common good refers to benefit to the body of Christ. As are all the gifts of the Spirit, discernment is given to build up the body to do the work of the ministry that is given to God's people. The gift of discernment is potentially resident within the church as it is needed. Discernment may be exercised by the entire body, or it may be resident within only one person. At times the gift is not given because the right conditions for discernment are not present. The gift of discernment is therefore "*potentially available to all of us.*" And when it is given *to* even one of us, it is given *for* all of us.

32. "*Spiritual discernment is a capacity to* see, *which is potentially available to all of us* that we may know God, and know God's will." This means seeing our lives clearly in the light of God's will so that we may live in the grace and truth of Jesus Christ.

33. The ultimate goal of spiritual discernment is to know God and Jesus Christ whom God sent (John 17:2). In other words, discernment results in a union of our wills with God's will. That is more than knowing of God generally or knowing about God distantly. It is knowing God, *will-fully*—so that my will is fully engaged in loving God. It is living in union with Jesus Christ.

34. Dr. Leslie Weatherhead's *The Will of God* has taught us how to appropriate three basic understandings about God's will: God's intentional will, circumstantial will, and ultimate will. (I have always wanted to add that God's primary will is that we know Jesus Christ as a saving and empowering presence.) This insight changed my attitude from fearing that God was out to get me, to beginning to think of God as *for* me (see Rom. 8:31). I could then understand that God loves me. Just think, the God of the universe loves *me*! (That fact is the greatest thing there is to know about me.) Therefore, it naturally follows that God wills the best for me—and for you—in any circumstance.

35. In the relationship God offers us, we participate in—and benefit from—what I think of as *general* wisdom that is available to us. When we need *general* wisdom, our discernment of God's will looks and feels like simply accepting the relationship that God offers, and loving God, and living in obedience to God with openness to the general flow of that will. We need *general* wisdom for everyday living, and it comes when we are living faithfully and tending to— and being tended by—the means of grace, which aid us in knowing and loving God. It can flow more naturally when we have had our minds stilled and our hearts made tender by prayer; when we are daily affirming our salvation in the way we live and love; when we feed on the Word; and when we gather regularly as the body. *General* wisdom is naturally and freely discerned as the fruit of a prayerful and committed life. As faithful Christians, we may expect that wisdom in our daily affairs. Most of the time *general* wisdom is sufficient for our needs.

36. But there is also *special* wisdom that we sometimes need when we encounter situations beyond our spiritual insight. On occasion, we may need more insight, more strength, more patience, or more love than is normally available to us.

37. We tend to think that discernment is limited to times when we face the big questions, the hard decisions, or the perplexing issues. Discernment is needed at such times, but to restrict it to extreme, and perhaps isolated, situations unnecessarily limits our experience and understanding of discernment and our relationship with God.

38. Isn't it as important to love God in all the little things as it is to know God's will in a few of the big—and perhaps more dramatic—things? If for no other reason than that we experience so many "ordinary" times, it may be even more important to know God's will during the everydays of life when general wisdom is adequate.

39. Reread paragraph 4 of the Introduction, pp. 9–10.

40. The promise of spiritual discernment is this: we can know and do God's will. God offers us an up-close and personal relationship. But we can never know God by studying God. We come to know God in the very process of our faithfulness to God—by doing God's will as we *know* it. The process stops if we are unfaithful to what we have *heard*, what we have *seen*, what we *know* to be God's will.

41. God does not play games with us as though the divine will were hidden and only God knows what it is. We do not have to sneak up on God or be clever enough to solve the riddle. If we love and walk with God, God and we create the path that leads to our awareness of the divine will *as we move along together*. Discerning God's will is living fully in the profoundly personal and fulfilling relationship with God that God offers us in Jesus Christ.

42. Spiritual discernment is a capacity to see our lives clearly in the light of God's will. This capacity is potentially available to all of us so that we may live our lives fully in the grace and truth of Jesus Christ. I do not mean to suggest by what I have said thus far that we require final, indisputable proof or clarity in each situation of our lives. Nor do I mean that we are given such insight prior to our commitment to live it out. After all, we are called to "walk by faith, not by sight." Nevertheless, God has shed divine light on our lives through Jesus Christ, and continues to do so by means of prayer, Scripture, and spiritual conversation. God yearns for us to be able to live according to the divine will and to know the fullness of our salvation in Jesus Christ. To this end, God has given us the means of grace, which make such a life possible.

Introduction to Week One and Week Two Exercises
Spiritual Discernment
in Decision Making

Welcome to Week One and Week Two of this workbook on spiritual discernment. Both weeks are presented together because they introduce spiritual discernment in decision making.

You can know God's will for your life! You can know whether a particular thing you have decided to do (or not to do) is God's will!

After reading the two narratives, you will be invited to select a need for discernment at a particular point in your life (Day 6). You will then be guided step-by-step through two classic methods of discernment in decision making: the Ignatian method and the Quaker Committee of Clearness.

By the end of Week Two, you will have a working knowledge of these two methods of discernment for use in making future decisions. You also will be well along the way to discerning God's will on your selected question/issue.

Follow the daily procedure carefully and you may end Week Two with two special gifts of insight: the best way for you to make decisions and the best way for you to be in church.

Spiritual Discernment in Decision Making

Day 1: My Best Advice to a 50-50 Person

READING

Read Narrative One.

REFLECTION AND RESPONSE

I learned some things as I looked back upon the accident crisis in my life. Think of one or more times when you may have faced a crisis and learned something significant as you looked back upon it. Name the crisis and list the lessons.

The crisis: _____

The Lessons _____

_____

_____

_____

Since now you may have more insight about this crisis than before, put an "N" by those that are new. Close your quiet time by thanking God that the crisis has taught you something beneficial. Sit in silence for two or three minutes, open to additional lessons to be gleaned from that crisis. Write here any new thoughts that come during the silence:

Day 2: Are You a 50-50 Person?

READING

Read again paragraph 15, p. 25.

REFLECTION AND RESPONSE

Are you a 50-50 person? Can you recall a time when a great loss consumed you? Are you facing such a situation now? If you are, think about what you are focusing on—the *better 50* or the *worse 50!* Write your thoughts here:

_____

_____

_____

_____

_____

_____

DO YOU KNOW ANY 50–50 PEOPLE?

Read again paragraph 18, p. 25.
Write the names of other 50–50 people here:

_____

_____

_____

Would there be value in your going to them to discuss the idea of concentrating on the *better 50* instead of the *worse 50*? If you are willing to talk with someone soon, write the name here, along with a target date.

Name of person _____ Target date _____

Read Mark 11:24. What does this verse mean to you?

_____

Spend the remainder of your devotional time today in silence and prayer. Reflect in your quiet time on how you will approach the person whose name you wrote above and what you will say. Pray earnestly for God's guidance about how to minister to that person.

Day 3: How Do You Feel About Ecstatic Experiences?

READING

Read again paragraphs 16–17, p. 25.
Read Luke 1:39–57

REFLECTION AND RESPONSE

Have you ever had an ecstatic experience, a trance, an overpowering emotion?

If your answer is yes, describe it here briefly: _____

_____

_____

_____

Do you tend to have such experiences regularly?
Yes____ No____

What would happen if you had to wait for an ecstatic experience to discern God's will for your life? Write your thoughts here:

_____

_____

_____

_____

We may have limited our discernment possibilities because we do not feel comfortable with "unworldly," "spiritual" experiences or feel free to talk about them.

From your reading of today's Scripture, do you think Elizabeth related to Mary out of an ecstatic experience or a "normal" experience?

Write your choice here: _____

_____

Now think about three specific areas of your life where you need to know God's will and write them here:

1. _____

2. _____

3. _____

Day 4: What Is the Difference?

READING

Read again paragraph 25, p. 27.
Read Acts 7:54–59.

REFLECTION AND RESPONSE

I began Narrative One and this workbook with the question, "What is spiritual discernment?"

It is a gift.

Principles are involved.

It can be ecstatic.

It also comes during our common experiences.

Discernment is for everyone.

Through discernment, you can know the will of God.

I discerned that God's will was for me to focus my life on my *better 50* instead of my *worse 50*. We all know that positive thinking is always preferred and that it promotes healing. So was this just a good idea (good), or was it a wonderful insight (better), or was it a spiritual discernment (best)? This has to do with the answer to the question "How deep did it go?" What do you think?

_____

_____

_____

_____

Day 5: A Difference Worth Knowing

READING

Read again paragraph 26, p. 27.

Read also Acts 7:54–59.

As you begin your reflection today, read again about Stephen in paragraph 25 on p. 13.

REFLECTION AND RESPONSE

There is a difference between a good idea, a wonderful insight, and spiritual discernment. The difference for me is revealed by the way I react to each of the three:

1. A good idea may change my thinking.
2. A wonderful insight may change my actions.
3. A spiritual discernment of God's will for my life goes right to the heart of my being and changes me!

Young Stephen had discerned God's will for himself. God's will was not that he should be stoned to death, but that regardless of his circumstance he would be faithful to God. How is that Scripture an example of No. 3 above? _____

_____

_____

You have probably discerned God's will for your life more often than you realize. Reflect upon this past year and list as many instances as you can recall of times you experienced a deep change in your life. List them here:

_____

_____

_____

_____

If you long for more such times in your life, you are in the right place and doing the right thing. We can all learn how to discern God's will. That is what we will consider on Day Six.

For now, close with a prayer for openness to the movement of the Holy Spirit in your life so that you may develop a discerning heart. Then go in peace!

Day 6: To Discern or Not to Discern

READING

Read Narrative Two, pp. 41ff.
Read again paragraphs 9–11, pp. 42–43.
Read Matthew 1:19–25.

REFLECTION AND RESPONSE

Not every question you face is a spiritual-discernment question. It takes discernment to know which questions are matters of spiritual discernment. If you are troubled about an issue, you probably should make it a matter for spiritual discernment.

Copy Fr. Green's three criteria here:

_____

_____

_____

As you select a particular question/issue for which you desire discernment, think of Joseph's perplexing situation and how he worked through it. Choose something significant on which you want spiritual discernment. Then apply the three criteria listed above to help in your discernment and to give you a working knowledge of these criteria.

Write your discernment question/issue here:

_____

Note: If you are having difficulty identifying a discernment question/issue, thinking harder probably won't help. Discernment will more likely come as you pray for insight about your situation. Thinking harder or trying harder are not so effective as prayer. While you pray, consider whether you should talk with your pastor or another trusted friend to help you clarify the question/issue.

As you prepare for tomorrow's workbook exercise, schedule adequate time to complete it before you go to church. Be seated in the sanctuary a few minutes early so that you will have some time for quality silence to focus on worship.

Day 7: A Commitment to Discern

It is important that you complete today's exercise before you go to church today.

READING

Read 1 Corinthians 12:12–31

REFLECTION AND RESPONSE

While you think about this Scripture, think of ways it relates to your being in church today. Write your thoughts here:

_____

_____

_____

_____

As you find yourself with the body of Christ today, you will have completed a circle that is necessary for spiritual discernment. Your personal discernment of God's will is enhanced as you share your gifts and receive the gifts of others within the body. Our personal discernment is intended to be validated within and through the community of faith.

The corporate nature of discernment is the sum total of personal spiritual sensitivity and openness to the Spirit of God within your congregation. Corporate and personal discernment are necessary, for they complete each other. *Why* you go to church and *how* you are in church is an expression of your love for God and of your openness to spiritual discernment. Name something you will do in church today that will enhance your ability to hear God. Write your intention here:

_____

_____

_____

Now is a good time to review the notes you have written this week. How do you feel about your journey? In the space below, jot down significant things you learned this week about:

Discernment in ordinary situations: _____

_____

The 50-50 person _____

_____

Personal discernment _____

_____

Corporate discernment _____

_____

Others _____

_____

Summarize your feelings about this first week _____

_____

Group Meeting Following Week One

The leader will plan the meeting to last no more than an hour and a half, arrange chairs in a circle, and welcome participants. Start on time.

 • Introduce everyone again and distribute name tags if needed.

FIRST: Invite participants to review their workbooks and select one or more of the following points to discuss (list on a chalkboard significant learnings from the entire group):
 • The most meaningful day of the week
 • A significant learning of the week
 • The discernment question/issue listed on Day Six
 • A particular Scripture relating to discernment
 • The 50-50 person
 • A question for the group to discuss now

 Leader: Help the group celebrate any "aha" experiences that are shared.

NEXT: How about your worship experience on Day 7?
 • How was worship different from previous Sundays?
 • What did the Scripture say to you?
 • How are you doing with silence?
 • What is your feeling (opinion) about discernment being for *everyone* as mentioned in the Introduction?

 Note: The implications of the Scripture on Day 7 are far-reaching. Our use of 1 Corinthians 12:12–31 on Day 7 of each week keeps before the group the importance of a biblical understanding of the church as the body of Christ. At each meeting, spend significant time discussing the images and lessons from that passage.

*   *   *

If you missed a day in the workbook this week, complete the exercise and be ready to move into Week Two. If you cannot complete what you missed before beginning Week Two, put it aside for now and begin the new week with renewed enthusiasm. Don't be discouraged by something you have missed, for there is much more to come. Tomorrow is a new day, a new week, and a new adventure in spiritual discernment. Don't miss it!

Pray together:

Does anyone have requests for prayer? (Ask participants to write requests in the front cover of their workbooks.)

Leader: "Let's join hands in our circle and pray in silence for two or three minutes, ending with the Lord's Prayer."

Spiritual Discernment for the Individual

1. He said, "I will meet you at the Iris Room at 11:30. We'll beat the crowd that way." The Iris Room was a good choice because it had a wonderful taco bar.

2. David, my 25-year-old son, didn't say much when he sat down with a couple of tacos. He seemed preoccupied just as he had when his mother talked to him by phone two days earlier. No, he didn't have a cold. Yes, his work was going fine. "Mom, I just have a lot on my mind," he had insisted. Did he ever!

3. I had invited him to lunch because I felt that both of us wanted to talk. Actually, I was following up on a conversation we had the day before when he suggested that we get together and talk about his exciting dreams of moving into more sophisticated and challenging financial management. I knew from a previous conversation that he was frustrated because of too many attractive choices facing him. The options were as impressive as they were bewildering:

(A) He had an excellent job with a leading financial management company.
   1) He had an opportunity to move to that firm's New York office.
   2) He had an offer to go with another firm on Wall Street.
   3) He could stay with his firm locally.

(B) He had a wonderful romance with Susan who would graduate soon as a registered nurse.
   1) He could marry her in the summer.
   2) He could postpone marriage in order to complete his career change.

His dilemma was that he wanted to do it all.

4. I said, "David, it is too much for Susan to graduate and take her state nursing exams, you to start a new job, her to start a new career, both of you to start a new marriage and a home (in New York

of all places) all in one summer. These are all wonderful possibilities, but timing is essential. Let's think primarily about processes for handling these questions and only incidentally about the facts and possibilities themselves.''

5. I mentioned that he was trying to make logical decisions about his career and, at the same time, make emotional decisions about his romance with Susan. These decisions were hard to reconcile and, therefore, he was confused. "Yes," he said, "so much is going on, it's very frustrating.''

6. I reminded him of the Academy for Spiritual Formation in which we seek to make decisions on a plane that is above logic— through spiritual discernment by consensus. The Academy's leadership team of six persons does not vote when it must resolve matters of concern. The group uses spiritual discernment by consensus to make corporate decisions that affect a large group of people. David needed individual, rather than corporate, discernment, but he saw that the consensus of others would be important as he made his decisions, even if consensus would be achieved differently. Obviously, he and Susan would both be involved in any decisions that were made, and consensus between them was essential. He agreed that they would expect their families, and perhaps a few selected friends, to enter the discerning process with them.

7. I said, "There are those happy occasions when either of two attractive alternatives could be lived out within the Spirit and love of God. At such times, it is as though God says, 'Take your pick of either choice and go live your life!' But there are also those difficult times when you experience anxiety and confusion. Perhaps you feel that way now." I proposed the higher method of spiritual discernment.

8. "It is important for you to know if there is a spiritual factor involved in these questions. Does God have anything to do with all of this? Is it even important to you to ask whether God's will is involved here? Since knowing and doing God's will is important to you" I said, "perhaps the approach to discernment in *Weeds Among the Wheat* by Thomas H. Green, S.J., which I have been reading, will be helpful. He describes the Ignatian method of decision making through discernment." St. Ignatius lived about 400 years ago. In his method of experiencing God, he gathered and distilled and synthesized spiritual training up to that time in history.

9. Father Green describes three conditions or criteria that must be present before spiritual discernment can occur:

1. A DESIRE TO DO THE WILL OF GOD

If one does not see how the will of God bears upon his or her situation, then the discernment process is not valued and decisions can be made on some other basis.

2. AN OPENNESS TO GOD

This is a precondition to knowing the will of God. It is not the same as saying, "I would like to know God's will, and if it corresponds with my will, I will do it." It is more like giving God a presigned check. It is a commitment to do God's will before it is revealed. Father Green says it is not God's will AND . . . or God's will IF . . . but God's will ONLY!

3. AN AWARENESS OF HOW GOD ACTS IN ORDER TO RECOGNIZE GOD'S ACTIONS

This suggests an experiential relationship with God—not just a secondhand relationship. The important question is: Are my feelings compatible with my ongoing experience of God or dissonant with what I know of God's ways?

10. "David, two more things are important in spiritual discernment. Sometimes we are faced with moral issues and do not know how to choose. God will help us to understand and make the right decisions if we ask for help. At other times, however, discernment does not involve choosing between right and wrong or good and evil. Whether I rob you or give to you are not spiritual discernment questions but moral questions. We discern God's will so we may choose the best." We talked about this for a little while.

11. "And the other thing that is important is that in spiritual discernment we do not seek God's favorite among several possibilities. We do not offer God a multiple-choice question. By using conventional methods of decision making we choose what we feel is the one best possibility among all the options and then, by spiritual discernment, we seek to determine whether it is God's will."

12. As we discussed it, we finally reduced his dilemma to two basic alternatives. First, he could follow his long-time personal dream for a career change and make it immediately. This would give Susan time to graduate, take her state boards, and get settled in her job. Then they could get married in six or eight months. Or, second, they could get married immediately, keep the stable and reliable income that the present job offered, start their marriage and their home, let Susan start her career in familiar surroundings—and then in six or eight months move to New York. Each alternative was good, but which was God's will for them?

13. David's dilemma was made more difficult by a third option that seemed so unworkable that when his married brother, Alan, heard it, he responded, "That's the dumbest idea I have ever heard." The idea David had been considering was to do it all this summer: Susan would finish school, take state boards, they would get married, move to New York, start new jobs and set up a new home.

14. I wanted to make it clear that in discerning God's will, you can't discern three choices or even two. It is essential to find the one choice that you feel is best. The other choices are eliminated—at least temporarily. With this one alternative chosen, the question then becomes, *"Is this the will of God for us?"* Yes or no?

15. Spiritual discernment questions are always yes or no questions, never choices among alternatives. If the answer is no, then any of the discarded choices may be retrieved or new ones found. Each one that is deemed worthy can still be tested: Is this the will of God? Yes or no?

16. Father Green described three situations that are both confused with and involved in spiritual discernment. Situation One is not properly discernment, but pure gift—St. Ignatius called it "revelation time." That is the situation in which something is so clear and unmistakable that there is no question to be discerned. Two classic examples are Paul's conversion on the road to Damascus and Jesus' calling of Levi to leave his tax tables and become Jesus' disciple. Those were not matters to be discerned. Each man immediately followed—no questions asked. Ignatius says that is pure grace and not an occasion for discernment.

17. Then Father Green talks about Situation Three, temporarily skipping over Situation Two. St. Ignatius called this third time "reasoning time." Here alternatives come into play. Since there are usually alternatives, evaluation is essential. So data are gathered, logic and hunches are considered. A decision is made to select one choice among the many. In making the choice, one utilizes all of the available research and cognitive evaluation, and uses the best tools and methods of decision making that are available.

18. And so Situation One is not discernment, it is pure grace. Nor is Situation Three actually discernment; it is conventional, everyday, garden-variety decision making.

19. After the decision has been made, one is ready for Situation Two, which is true spiritual discernment. In Situation Two, one offers the selected choice to God in prayer and patiently asks, "Is this the will of God?" Yes or no? One earnestly searches for God's will to be revealed, and has made a prior commitment to do God's will when it is known. The choice is offered in patience because one cannot hurry a thing like that. It often takes time—at least one should be prepared to wait and listen in patience.

20. "David, here is a critical point in the discernment process. You will know that the answer is either yes or no according to the feeling you get. You do not discern facts. You evaluate facts. Feelings are important here. St. Ignatius said that in time the Holy Spirit gives one of only two responses—the feeling of *consolation* or the feeling of *desolation*. Both feelings may occur simultaneously, but in time one will become dominant.

21. "Consolation is like peace, freedom. Consolation is the joy that comes when you think about that decision. It is a wonderful, free feeling. When suddenly you think about your decision again, lightness and rightness surround it. Desolation is a troubled, ill-at-ease feeling, heaviness, the absence of peace and joy, darkness. Instead of freedom, you feel stifled. It does not feel right. In time, either consolation or desolation will prevail."

22. "Perhaps you are clearly in Situation Three. You will have to decide which choice will be most fulfilling. Which will be most important to you twenty years from now? Should you immediately pursue your long-held professional plans and then work marriage into them? Or do you choose marriage and subordinate, or perhaps alter, your professional plans? You can't do both at the same time.

23. "I want to tell you about the Quaker way of handling a difficult decision. I believe they call it a *Committee of Clearness*. Ask three or four people who are mature and who know and love you to serve as a clearness committee for you. They are not to make decisions for you nor even advise you. It is difficult for people you take into your confidence to resist the temptation to tell you what they would do or to tell you what you ought to do. That is why it is so important to have mature friends on a Committee of Clearness.

24. "Once you have your Committee of Clearness, write a brief paragraph or two describing the issue you are facing. Give it to them when they come together. Then you ask, as though you were qualifying a jury, whether any of them have experienced something that would make objectivity difficult or impossible. This is important because it is not their will but God's will you are trying to discern. If anyone feels biased, that person must be excused. Those remaining take your question as a deliberate prayer concern until the next meeting. It is gratifying to know that they are praying with you. There is great power in intercessory prayer and the prayer of the Committee of Clearness is intercessory prayer at its best. At an agreed time, you meet the committee again. Remember, they cannot give advice or advocate a particular solution. They may only ask probing questions for you to consider. Unhurriedly, lovingly, they ask the deep and hard questions without evaluating or criticizing your answers. Through prayer and love for you, under the guidance of the Holy Spirit, they help you consider the questions from every side. This meeting will probably be marked with significant periods of silent reflection while your answers are offered and additional questions are framed. When the committee's questions have been answered, all go their way for another period of prayer. Clarity is expected to come! It might come in one meeting or require several. When clearness comes, you thank the group, and the Committee of Clearness is dissolved. You have friends who would be happy to act as a Committee of Clearness for you. *You don't have to be alone in this.*"

25. David's faraway look finally broke as he looked at me with a faint smile. I was glad that I had had opportunity to describe for him the two best helps I knew in spiritual discernment. Another deep feeling was a sense of pain for my son as we rode down the escalator to leave.

26. It's tough making decisions. As I walked to the car, I was clear about one thing: Knowing Susan as I did, I would not have difficulty choosing between career goals or a relationship with her. But I was glad that I had remained faithful in my luncheon promise not to offer advice—but to talk only about ways to handle difficult decisions.

27. David and Susan told us one night not long afterward that he had asked her to marry him. While sitting at the same table where they had their first dinner together seven months earlier, she said yes. Discernment had come. The circle was complete. Such a beautiful diamond. Such a beautiful couple. And there was, and remains, such a wonderful feeling of *consolation* for Susan and David, and for both of us!

Making Discernment Personal

Day 1: What Is the Question?—Part 1

READING

Read again the workbook content of Day Six of the last unit (see p. 36) and pay special attention to what you wrote on that day.

REFLECTION AND RESPONSE

Did you designate a discernment issue/question as called for on Day 6? If you did, great, because there is no need to proceed until that is done.

Copy your discernment issue/question here:

_____

Remember now, you have written only your discernment issue/question, not your solution/answer, which we will consider tomorrow.

Here is the simple pattern you will follow to involve you in the Ignatian method of discernment:

1. What is the issue?
2. What is your best solution/answer to it?
3. Pray about the best solution/answer until you feel:
    a. Consolation, i.e., a sense of ease, inner strength, calm; or
    b. Desolation, i.e., anxiety, confusion, or agitation.

Let's follow this pattern using the discernment issue you wrote above.

Evaluate what you wrote on Day Six by using these three criteria: (1) Are you asking the right question? (2) Have you selected the one best solution to present to God for spiritual discernment? (3) Are you open to God and ready for spiritual discernment? We will explore these criteria during the next few days.

(1) ASK THE RIGHT QUESTION

Since most significant issues can be complicated by several potential solutions, it is important to determine whether you are facing a moral question or a discernment question. Any solution/answer that is decided on the basis of good or evil, right or wrong is a moral question. You can discern only between two goods, never between a good and a bad. If your issue/question involves solutions/answers that are good, you are on the right track. Each *good* choice may become a matter of spiritual discernment.

When you feel that this condition has been met (that your question is a discernment issue and not a moral question) *pray* about the issue/question you listed on Day 6. Remember, nothing can substitute for prayer and quiet listening for God throughout your process of discernment. Pray and meditate upon the issue you wrote on the blank above to make certain that you have stated it as simply as possible. Pray about it now before you go.

Day 2: What Is the Question?—Part 2

READING

Read again paragraphs 13–15, pp. 43–44.

"If the answer is no, then any of the discarded choices may be retrieved or new ones found. Each one that is deemed worthy can still be tested, 'Is this the will of God?' Yes or no?" (paragraph 15)

Read also 1 Samuel 16:1–13.

REFLECTION AND RESPONSE

(2) NO MULTIPLE CHOICE ANSWERS, PLEASE

As you think of the issue/question that you wrote on Day 6, you may discover several solutions/answers for it. Select the one best solution/answer to test through spiritual discernment. It is necessary that you come to a single solution/answer because in discernment we do not present God with multiple-choice questions.

Since this is a major discernment issue/question for you, I assume that you have prayed about it before today. If, and when, you have selected what you feel is the best solution/answer for the issue/question you wrote on Day 6, write it here and proceed:

_____

_____

Now *you want to discern whether it is God's will.*

Do not try to move too rapidly here. Before you go, spend a few minutes in silence to think about what you have done so far. Technically, Criterion No. 2 involves decision making. That is a necessary part of discernment, but is not actually spiritual discernment in the truest sense.

Pray about your relationship with God and the discernment of God's will that you desire. The Lord told Samuel that the Lord looks upon the heart (v. 7). That is true for you and me also!

Day 3: Are You Ready for Discernment?

READING

Read paragraphs 10–11, p. 43.
Also read paragraph 7, p. 42.
Read Acts 1:21–26

REFLECTION AND RESPONSE

How does the passage from Acts relate to the workbook content you reviewed today?

_____

_____

_____

Not every question is a discernment question. It may sometimes be easier (and quicker) to settle an issue on some other basis than through spiritual discernment. If you can resolve the matter and feel good about the decision, that is OK. But your big issue is, "Is it important that I know God's will on this question?" Do not be casual about that in an effort to save time.

You may have the happy experience of encountering two wonderful alternatives that are equally attractive to you, as did the disciples in the Scripture from Acts. It may be God's will for you to "Take your pick and go live your life."

If you have prayed it through and feel a deep peace about both options, you may be ready to take your pick. But before you do, ask a spiritual friend to take your situation as a prayer concern. Discuss his or her feelings of consolation or desolation. Don't be impetuous. Only when you can act with peace are you free to take your pick and go live your life!

Day 4: Test Yourself

READING

Read Matthew 7:21–27.

REFLECTION AND RESPONSE

(3) THE BIG TEST

Your discernment issue is ready, but the question is, *are you ready?* Evaluate yourself and your openness and readiness for spiritual discernment.

Test yourself on the particular question/issue that you wrote in the blank during Day 1 of this unit by praying about and thinking through the following criteria for discernment. No hasty answers, please! This is the big test to help you know whether you are ready for spiritual discernment on this matter.

On this question/issue:

(a) Do you have a desire to do the will of God?

(b) Do you have an openness (a predisposition) to do God's will in this matter before you know what God's will is?

(c) Will you recognize God's actions? (That is, do you have an ongoing experience of God so you will know whether the actions you perceive are compatible with the way God acts?)

During a period of silence, reflect on your question/issue with three criteria (the two from Days 1 and 2 and the one today) in mind.

This is the first Big Test in spiritual discernment. Are you open to discernment of God's will?

> **Note:** The discernment question/issue you wrote during Day 1 of this unit will continue to be the focus of additional steps in discernment for the next two days. If you find that there is a more important discernment question/issue for you, substitute it, and follow through with it on the procedure described above.

Keep your question/issue and answer/solution, which you wrote during Day 2 of this unit, as a continuing matter of prayer so that you may know God's will for you now.

Day 5: One Way to Discern

READING

Read paragraphs 16–21, pp. 44–45.

Read also Acts 9:1–9.

REFLECTION AND RESPONSE

All who have had a "revelation time," as Father Green describes it, may rejoice. It is a beautiful experience, but rare.

Let's look at the other two—reasoning time and discernment time—as you think again about your discernment question/issue listed earlier. Write your current version of the question/issue for which you need discernment (see Day 1 of this unit):

_____

Have you taken the necessary steps in "reasoning time" to choose your best solution/answer? Have you gathered adequate information? Have you consulted sufficiently if consultation is indicated or needed? Here are the steps in ordinary decision-making:
(1) Information gathering
(2) Consultation
(3) Consideration (reflection and prayer)
(4) Decision

Now write your current, best answer/solution here:

_____

If you are satisfied that this is the best answer/solution up to now, go directly to "discernment time." *You do that by offering to God in prayer the alternative you have chosen to ask whether this is God's will for you.*

Pray earnestly! Wait in patience! There is no way to hurry discernment. Do not try to complete your praying about this matter before the end of today, or this week, or even this month.

To pray and wait in patience does not suggest long prayers or long periods of silence and meditation. Pray brief prayers, followed by brief periods of silence. You will know when discernment comes. Pray often. Wait patiently.

The discernment process is often an extended prayer experience in many parts. You should not expect an automatic computer "printout" answer to your prayers. When you have ended your prayer time for now, read again about consolation and desolation (page 45). When consolation comes, go with it.

If desolation comes to you over a period of time, you will want to reread about decision making in what St. Ignatius called "reasoning time" (page 44). Select another of the *good* alternatives/solutions, and work through the suggested steps of decision making until you have a *good* answer/solution to test by prayerful discernment.

Open yourself to God in the silence before you go today!

Day 6: Another Way to Discern

READING

Read paragraphs 23–24, p. 45.
Read Acts 9:10–22.

REFLECTION AND RESPONSE

On Day 5, we used the Ignatian method to explore your discernment question/issue.

Today, we will consider the Quaker Committee of Clearness as another method of discernment. If you choose to experiment with this approach, select your Committee of Clearness.

How does today's Scripture illustrate the way "clearness" came to Paul?

_____

_____

_____

For now, it will be helpful for you to write a simple statement describing the issue/question listed on Day 5 about which you are unclear. (This is the same issue/question that you considered in the Ignatian method.)

Be prayerful as you write your statement on a separate piece of paper. Write no more than a single handwritten page (if possible) and express yourself as simply and as completely as you can. (Except for a closing time of silence, this is the only feature in the remainder of this period, so take your time in writing your statement.) Then return to this workbook for a closing invitation.

You have been introduced to two classical discernment methods that you may find useful. Select the discernment method (either the Ignatian method or the Quaker Committee of Clearness) that you are ready to use and proceed with it. Which method of discernment did you choose?_____

_____

Put no timetable on this project, except the *time of beginning*.

There is no substitute for your faithful follow-through on the method you have chosen.

As you prepare for tomorrow's workbook exercise, schedule adequate time to begin the exercise before you go to church. Be seated in the sanctuary a few minutes early so you will have a good time of silence to focus on worship.

Day 7: As You Go To Church Today

> **Note:** It is important to begin today's exercise before you go to church today. Then return to your workbook to complete the exercise.

READING

Read 1 Corinthians 12:12–31
Read Luke 22:24–27.

REFLECTION AND RESPONSE

While in church today, be aware—in a discerning way—of the people you see. Welcome everyone. You will support the spiritual quality of the service by being a spiritual presence. There is also the spirituality of relationships. *See if you can make a spiritual difference in church today.*

While in church, also look for one special person—someone who understands and practices the life described by the four verses of today's Scripture from Luke. Read those verses again now. Before you leave, thank God for that individual, for he or she is a vital spiritual force in your church. Write the person's name here:

_____

How does that person measure up to the passage from 1 Corinthians 12:12–31? Write your thoughts here:

_____

_____

_____

Remember that person, for he or she is your colleague in spiritual discernment. Such persons have already been discerning the will of God for themselves and their communities.

Don't forget to return to your workbook to complete this assignment after church.

Group Meeting Following Week Two

The leader will plan the meeting to last no more than an hour and a half, arrange chairs in a circle, and welcome participants. Start on time.

- Begin the meeting with five minutes of silence for each individual to reflect upon the contents of the workbook and experiences with discernment in the past week.
- End the silence with a spoken prayer for the group to be open to each other and to the Holy Spirit.
- Ask about the relevance to your group of 1 Corinthians 12:12–31.

FIRST: Invite participants to review their workbooks and select one or more of the following points to discuss:
- The most meaningful day of the week
- Something significant learned during the week
- A question for the group to discuss now
- A particular Scripture that needs to be discussed
- Questions or comments about the Ignatian method of discernment or the Committee of Clearness

NEXT: Ask a volunteer to summarize the major points of the Ignatian method of discernment in decision making.
It is important that everyone clearly understands this classical, simple model.
- After the summary, call for discussion and clarification.
- In groups of two, partners may benefit by summarizing the Ignatian method for each other.
- Invite members of the group to share their experiences with the Ignatian method.

THEN: Ask someone to describe the process of the Committee of Clearness.
- If it is not clear to everyone, ask groups of two to review the steps and summarize them for each other.
- Ask for volunteers to read the one-page statements they prepared for their Committees of Clearness.
- Ask whether everyone has selected one of the two models to use with a real life question/issue.

Note: It is crucial that participants go beyond superficial learnings about spiritual discernment. To read about it is a good thing; to experience it is better. This week's daily exercises are for real, and the concepts will be significant for the person who is serious about wanting to discern God's will.

FINALLY: How about your worship experience on Day 7?
- How did it differ from previous Sundays?
- What did the two Scripture passages say to you?
- How are you doing with silence?
- In our church, what possibilities do you see for using the Ignatian method of discernment or the Committee of Clearness?

During the coming week we shall look at the human side of discernment as we consider *Spiritual Intuition* during the first part of Week Three. Near the end of Week Three and in Week Four we shall also consider *How God Communicates*.

If you missed a day in the workbook this week, try to complete the exercise and be ready to move into Week Three.

Leader: Read the introduction to Week Three pattern exercises on page 60.

Let's pray together:

Before we call for requests for prayer, let's hear reports on any of the concerns we prayed about last week. Let's join hands in our circle and pray in silence for two or three minutes, ending with the Lord's Prayer.

Spiritual Intuition

1. Rosalie and I were privileged to spend some vacation days on the island of Kauai in Hawaii to celebrate our fiftieth wedding anniversary. We had been married only twenty-seven years, but we decided to celebrate our fiftieth while we were there since we did not know where we would be when that day actually came.

2. On the very first afternoon, we had a remarkable encounter with a different kind of spiritual discernment—spiritual intuition. We decided to go shopping in the colorful hotel shops. I was eager to get a Hawaiian shirt but not just a colorful shirt. I deserved an elegantly colored shirt. I had passed over several and was on my way to making a final choice when Rosalie said, "Let's go to the beach."

3. "Help me select my shirt and I'll wear it to the beach," I said.

4. "No," she insisted, "we can look for a shirt later." She took two shirts out of my hands, laid them aside and led me out of the store against my protests. "Come on, I want to go to the beach."

5. Surprisingly, the beach was almost deserted, unusual for 6:00 on a beautiful Saturday afternoon. We saw just one woman and a man. The man ran down the beach leaving the woman alone. We were perhaps fifty yards from her. She seemed to be shouting at us, but we could not hear her. Suddenly we heard her scream frantically, "My husband is drowning!"

6. I sprinted toward the hotel for help. Rosalie ran toward the traffic and stopped a car. The two motorists dashed across the road and charged into the roaring surf. By the time I returned from the hotel with help, they had pulled the man to the shore. Rosalie, who is a registered nurse, was bent over the man's inert form, applying mouth-to-mouth resuscitation.

7. He had already turned blue around the mouth and in his hands and feet. We were losing! A doctor rushed up and quickly sized up the situation. "We have about 15 seconds," he declared as he applied oxygen. Then he began to pump the victim's chest. "Breathe!" he urged. "Come on, man, breathe!"

8. And, miraculously, the man did breathe. He gasped for air, then gasped again. By the time the ambulance arrived he was breathing on his own, and color was returning to his face and limbs.

9. Talk about providential care! God providing in miraculous ways! Consider this list of provisions:

- We were the only persons on the beach, except for the man's wife and a passerby she had sent for help. (He had run in the wrong direction.)
- Rosalie is a registered nurse and trained in CPR.
- The two men she flagged down (the only car that stopped) were native to that island and were young, expert swimmers. They were also EMTs.
- If I had not run to the hotel, we would not have had the oxygen.
- The doctor who ran out to help was a cardiologist.

10. Coming down to the wire with fifteen seconds to go, if I had looked at one more shirt it would have been too late! We were awed by the uncanny sequence of events laid end-to-end like dominoes. What began as a leisurely shopping expedition turned into an unforgettable afternoon. As I recall this experience, I realize that at the time I was not particularly surprised by Rosalie's out-of-the-blue insistence that we go to the beach. Often I have had to wonder whether she was standing in light I could not see or just being stubborn. But she is also spiritually intuitive.

11. Spiritual intuition is not the same as stubbornness and I detected something special about Rosalie's insistence that we go to the beach that day. Intuition is a direct knowledge or awareness of something without conscious attention or reasoning; non-intellectual perception. Nothing innately spiritual is either stated or implied in that definition. But when a person allows the Holy Spirit to take control of his or her natural intuition, the result is spiritual intuition. Discernment through spiritual intuition provides a deeper understanding and expands the boundaries of awareness.

12. Since this episode occurred, I have been trying to sort out the meaning of what happened on the beach that day. My mind keeps going back to the abundant evidence of God's providential care.

13. But there is something more profound than the unusual events on the beach. I am intrigued by the question: *Where was God that day?* Is it fair to say that God was not on the beach—only a couple of EMTs, a nurse, a doctor, and a few other helpers?

14. Perhaps God's will was mediated in two parts: (1) God communicated; (2) human beings responded. Would that make God's communication in the shirt shop the sum total of God's intervention? Could it be that God was actually involved only at the one point where *God communicated*?

15. It is clear that God communicated and a human being with a sensitive spiritual intuition processed what God communicated. That does not diminish God's part. Rather, it suggests a strategy God uses much of the time: God teams up with us and relies upon human beings to respond to divine promptings through redemptive acts. The communication was the pivotal point of everything that followed and the intuitive response was teamwork and God's providential care at their highest level.

16. Those ministries of care on the beach were essential. But they seem less dramatic to me than God's act of communication and Rosalie's response to that communication in the shirt shop. That was the most phenomenal event of that day. *To think that God could put an idea into someone's mind and that person could comprehend that idea and immediately act upon it with unquestioning determination is the most remarkable wonder of all!*

17. A second wonder is that God has given all of us this capacity. God communicates with all of us! We get little nudges—feelings that this or that should be done or not done; we get hunches and leadings, signs and signals, and sometimes direct messages.

18. Each time I have told of our experience, people have come to tell me about similar experiences when God communicated with them. Their almost-embarrassed accounts of these instances suggest that they view such occurrences as extraordinary, strange, and suspect. But it would be more extraordinary if God did not communicate with us in this manner, for communication is part of God's nature. Teamwork with us is one of God's goals.

19. What is unusual is the ability of some of us to perceive God's communication clearly through spiritual intuition, and then to have the courage to honor the perception when it comes. "Courage" involves risk—even gambling—to follow one's leading when it comes out of a faith stance. The willingness to honor one's spiritual intuition is a measure of one's faithfulness. It is not the communication by God that is usually missing. Nor is it our ability to perceive it. We have to face our unwillingness to be faithful to what we know God is communicating. Our continued refusal to obey the promptings of God's Spirit clouds our ability to perceive what God communicates.

20. The next time you experience spiritual intuition, put away your worry about what others will think. Instead, consider your leading carefully. Test your leading with a spiritual friend. Ask the Holy Spirit to protect you, and then go as far as love will allow. God will bless your faithfulness.

21. *That God communicates* is the focus of this narrative. *How God Communicates* is the subject of Narrative 4.

Introduction to Week Three and
Week Four Exercises

The Human Side of Spiritual Discernment

Welcome to Week Three and Week Four of this workbook.

Discernment has two terminus points—you and God. For two weeks we shall look at the human capacities you bring to the experience of discernment.

During the coming week we shall examine spiritual intuitions as described in Narrative Three. Everyone has the capacity for spiritual intuition, although some people are more aware of it and open to it than others. Our obedience to the messages that come through spiritual intuition is a key to cultivating it.

In Week Four we shall consider how God communicates. No matter how or what God communicates, you can miss it by not using your human faculties for perceiving God's communication. When we reach Week Four, you will have opportunities to experience and to experiment with several of your natural capacities to discern.

The Human Side of Spiritual Discernment

Day 1: Spiritual Intuition

READING

Read Narrative Three, *Spiritual Intuition.*

REFLECTION AND RECORDING

We have studied two classical methods of spiritual discernment—the Ignatian, which is personal, and the Quaker Committee of Clearness, which is corporate.

Spiritual intuition is a third option for discernment that is available to us. Spiritual intuition is not so much a method we must learn as it is a capacity we need to develop. We are already endowed with natural intuition and use it frequently. But the Holy Spirit can enhance our natural intuition far beyond what we can anticipate or imagine. Such spiritual intuition provides a powerful facility for spiritual discernment.

Have you ever had an experience, whether more or less dramatic, like the one described in Narrative Three? How did you feel about it? Did you tell anyone? If you told, did that person wonder about you? Did you wonder about yourself? Do you suspect that intuitive experiences like this are rare? Would you immediately label such an experience "spiritual discernment"? Record on a separate piece of paper your reflections about spiritual intuition in your own life.

Day 2: How Does Spiritual Intuition Look to You?

READING

Read paragraphs 13–15, pp. 57–58.
Read Luke 4:1–13.

REFLECTION AND RESPONSE

Spiritual intuition is "a direct knowledge or awareness of something without conscious attention or reasoning; non-intellectual perception."

How is this passage from Luke an example of this definition?

_____

_____

How do you feel about this possibility in your life? Have you ever experienced "non-intellectual perception"? If your answer is yes, describe an experience here: _____

_____

_____

_____

If your answer is no, are you open to an experience of "non-intellectual perception"? Write your thoughts here: _____

_____

_____

Day 3: God Communicates!

READING

Read paragraphs 16–20, pp. 58–59.
Read 1 Corinthians 2.

REFLECTION AND RESPONSE

What does this passage from 1 Corinthians say about the human side of spiritual discernment? _____

_____

Do you believe that *God can put an idea into your mind and that you can comprehend that idea and immediately act upon it with unquestioned determination?* It is true! You now have that capacity!

Yesterday you were asked to recall such an experience. Can you think of another? Write a description of it here: _____

_____

Have you ever sensed little nudges or feelings that this or that should be done or not done? How about hunches and leadings, signs and signals? Direct messages? On the lines below list some examples of communication from God to you in any of these categories.

Nudges _____

Feelings _____

Hunches and leadings _____

Signs and signals _____

Direct messages _____

If you have been able to recall one or more examples in some or all of these categories, you have experienced the gift of spiritual intuition.

The big question to reflect on now is, have you acted on these communications? If you cannot recall any examples, you may need help understanding how God communicates. Tomorrow's session covers this subject.

Review your findings during a period of silence, ending with a prayer of thanksgiving for what you have learned today.

Day 4: How God Communicates

READING

Read Narrative Four, *How God Communicates*, pp. 70ff.
Read Acts 1:21–26.
Read Judges 6:36–40.

REFLECTION AND RESPONSE

To discern who should replace Judas, the disciples employed a method that for us is unusual: they drew lots. Was this only an ancient form of lottery or was it an instance of having to choose between two goods? Was this a dangerous method or an example of God's saying, "Take your pick and move on"?

Write your thoughts about the disciples' using the practice of casting lots as a discernment process. _____

_____

_____

Gideon put out a *fleece* before battling with the Midianites. He said to God, "If thou wilt deliver Israel by my hand, as thou hast said. . . ." (Judg. 6:36). In other words, prove it!

Have you ever put out a fleece? Have you ever prayed, "If *this* happens or *that* happens, then I will know your answer"? Think about your experiences and your prayers over a long period of time, and write your thoughts:

_____

_____

_____

Did you make the condition as hard as Gideon did (fleece wet— ground dry, etc.) or did you make the condition easy—for example, "If I am supposed to talk with that person, give me a sign by letting us cross paths"? Think about it and write your thoughts here:

_____

How is putting out a fleece as Gideon did, a form of discernment? _____

_____

Spend some time in silence and think about whether you do—or should—put God to the test as Gideon did.

Day 5: Examining Your Prayer Life to Learn How God Communicates With You

READING

Read the group exercise described on page 68.
Read Luke 11:5–13.

REFLECTING AND RECORDING

Here is a simple way to use this group activity as a personal exercise. Try to recall five or more prayer experiences that were special to you. List them here with a brief word that will remind you of each.

_____

_____

_____

_____

_____

_____

_____

_____

Now, beside each prayer experience, write one of the following words to designate the "port of entry" God used to communicate with you during that particular prayer time: mind, memory, emotion, will, imagination, or body. If more than one port of entry was involved, choose the strongest one.

Next, tally up the total number of times God used each faculty and compare it with the typical result described in the paragraph you read at the beginning of this session. Write your comparison here:

_____

_____

What does this comparison tell you about your prayer life?

_____

_____

What does the passage from Luke say about your prayer life?

_____

_____

_____

Day 6: Emotion

READING

Read about emotion beginning on page 71.
Read 1 Kings 19:11–13

REFLECTION AND RESPONSE

If understanding emotion in your life as a Christian has been a problem for you, read again the four inaccurate conclusions, listed on page 71, that many well-meaning people have about emotion. Put a check mark in the parentheses by the number(s) of any of the four that expresses the way you actually feel.

1 ( ) _____

2 ( ) _____

3 ( ) _____
4 ( ) _____

Then, on the line beside each number you checked, write anything positive you can about that attitude.

When you are finished, consider whether Elijah's experience of the storm, whirlwind, fire, and "still small voice" informs you about the involvement of emotion in encounters with God.

As you prepare for tomorrow's session, schedule time to complete the exercise before you go to church. Be seated there a few minutes early so you will have a time of silence to focus on worship.

Day 7: You, in the Body of Christ

NOTE: It is important to begin this exercise before you go to church today. Plan now to return to your workbook after church because part of the exercise will be completed after your time of worship.

READING

First, read 1 Corinthians 12:12–31.
Read paragraphs 30–31, Narrative 4, page 75.

REFLECTION AND RESPONSE

> **NOTE:** This Scripture from 1 Corinthians is the same passage you have been reading each Sunday. There is value in rereading it, so do not skip the reading simply because you know what it is about. Each time we read this passage, we will consider it from a different point of view.

Review your workbook for Day 7 of last week.

As you sit in church today, pay close attention to people. Whether you know all of them or not, they are important people in your life, for they and you together make up the body of Christ described in the Scripture you just read. That means that they are *your* body of Christ. They are important to you in your spiritual journey, and you are important to them in theirs.

When you need spiritual guidance, consider these three steps:

FIRST, look for guidance in Scripture.

NEXT, look for guidance in the context of your own personal spiritual orientation.

FINALLY, ask for spiritual guidance through members of your body of Christ. Meet with a special Christian friend to talk over your Day 3 list of nudges, feelings, hunches, and leadings. Explain why you wrote that list, and discuss it with your friend.

Do you see someone in church today with whom you would feel free to talk about spiritual guidance? If so, write his or her name here: _____

Don't forget to return to your workbook to complete the exercise.

Group Meeting Following Week Three

The leader will plan the meeting so that it will last no more than an hour to an hour and a half, arrange chairs in a circle, and be present to welcome participants. Start on time.

FIRST: Invite participants to review their workbooks and select one or more of the following points to talk about:
- The most meaningful session of the week
- A significant learning of the week
- A question for the group to discuss now
- A particular Scripture that needs to be discussed
- The Ports of Entry
- A discussion of 1 Corinthians 12

THE HUMAN SIDE OF SPIRITUAL DISCERNMENT has been the theme for this week. By week's end all participants should be clear about the following:
1) Spiritual discernment is not complicated.
2) Specific methods or practices are helpful.
3) Spiritual discernment is possible for *everyone* who practices the principles of discernment.
4) The fact that there is a human side of spiritual discernment is a great affirmation for any person.
5) God is more eager to communicate the divine will to us than we are to discern it!

Spiritual Intuition

- Invite participants to observe five minutes of group silence to recall a time when they experienced spiritual intuition. Or they may recall a time that, in retrospect, they now realize was spiritual intuition.
- After the silence, ask volunteers to share such an experience.
- The Big Question: Have you acted upon your spiritual intuitions? Poll the group for recollections of intuitions acted upon and not acted upon. Results? Regrets? Resolves?

Let's remember that everyone has experiences of spiritual intuition. Our awareness of these experiences and the way we value and appropriate them determines how we respond to God's leading.

Let's pray together:

Ask for reports on prayer requests from last week or the week before. Instruct participants to write significant learnings in their workbooks.

Talk about the practice of silence. Receive responses and encourage participants to practice silence in prayer and meditation.

Ask the group to sit in silence for five minutes.

Close with The Lord's Prayer.

How God Communicates

1. Perhaps nothing is more vital in spiritual discernment than to know that God *does* communicate and to know *how* God communicates. That God does communicate with us was never my question. But for a long time I wondered *how* God communicates with us. Father John Powell, S.J., helped me greatly in my understanding of spiritual discernment with his insight that God communicates with us through "ports of entry" into our consciousness: He names five ports of entry: the mind, emotion, imagination, memory, and will.

2. I have explored this concept with dozens of groups in The Adventure of Living Prayer, a retreat model sponsored by The Upper Room and developed by Maxie Dunnam and me. In The Adventure we utilize the film "An Act of Love" in which Fr. Powell illustrates the five ports of entry. After showing the film, I write these ports of entry on the chalkboard and ask participants (who are divided into groups of three) to recall a meaningful prayer experience and to think about which port of entry God used to communicate.

3. Can you remember when prayer became more for you than merely saying words? When did you deliberately claim the relationship of not only being called a child of God but of really *being* a child of God? Share with the others in your group the time *when you experienced for yourself a vital relationship with God in prayer.*

4. I am always impressed with how quickly participants recall their "He-touched-me" experience. Once they have done that, it is easy to take the next step: Identify to your group which port of entry God used to speak to you. More than one port may have been involved, but for the sake of our group exercise, designate only one.

5. After their discussion, I call for votes by precincts from around the room. Each person in a group designates his or her port of entry. I have done this with more than fifty groups. The result is remarkable in that it follows a predictable pattern. Typically, "emotion" is always first; "mind" is usually second but sometimes third; "will" is usually third but sometimes second; and "memory" and "imagination" always compete for fourth and fifth places. I have never found an exception to this pattern, no matter how large or small the group.

Emotion

6. When I ask the group what this pattern tells us, the immediate and invariably apologetic conclusion is that it reveals we are emotional people. I am saddened that many of the participants are ashamed of our emotional nature. They assume that to be emotional is to be weak, and the worst "case" of emotion they can imagine is religious emotion. They also assume that emotion in religion connotes sadness, guilt, or remorse. They seldom talk of emotion in religion as joy and celebration. Here are four other inaccurate conclusions well-meaning people have come to believe about emotion in religion:

(1) Emotion is caused only by religious excess.
(2) If you open yourself up to emotions, you may not know know to handle the situation.
(3) An emotional response suggests that one has lost control.
(4) The person and/or the group might be embarrassed by "an emotional outburst."

7. The church must address these negative attitudes about emotion in religion. Head religion and heart religion cannot flourish without each other. Separately, they only reproduce themselves, while together they produce Christian maturity.

Imagination

8. My next question to the group is, Why does "imagination" get so few votes (usually two or three out of forty or fifty)? When I begin to answer my rhetorical question by telling a part of my own story, I see nods of agreement all over the room.

9. As a child, I was trained not to use my imagination. As a first or second grader, I was scolded for daydreaming instead of doing my work. Letting one's mind wander was a no-no. I was told that if my mind wandered, I would soon be fantasizing, and fantasy is dangerous: "You could go off the deep end if you are not careful." After all, I had work to do and I had to be productive. How many times was I told that an idle mind is the devil's workshop? I was introduced only to models that were "productive." My high school curriculum offered a smattering of poetry and no art at all. Great literature was never held up as a source of food for my imagination.

10. Later the Protestant work ethic took over. The message was clear: "Be productive so you will amount to something." "Get ahead!" "A good day's work for a good day's pay." "Go early and stay late." You are valued by the work you do!"

11. Imagination and creativity were spurned and ridiculed. When at times someone chose not to be gainfully employed (and I don't mean just leisure), he or she was said to be strange or different—a sluggard.

12. Imagine my shock when at forty years of age I visited Disney World for the first time and found myself walking through the park with childlike intrigue. Everything I saw was fascinating and colorful and creative. Everywhere I looked I saw sheer fantasy. It was wonderful! I loved it! Everyone loved it!

13. That day at Disney World I made a discovery: All those people who told me that fantasy was bad and must be avoided at any price were wrong. Fantasy is good. It is creative imagination at work and creative imagination is a gift of God.

14. When I ask a group, "Were any of you reared as I was?" people of all ages identify with me.

15. We are crippled in our ability to "hear" God communicate with us when we squelch creative imagination. How many songs are unsung, thoughts trampled, visions not seen because we fail to use and to develop our God-given creative imagination?

Memory

16. When we consider memory as a port of entry through which God communicates with us, participants in The Adventure of Living Prayer are usually puzzled. I suppose most people think of memory as our ability to recall dates, facts, telephone numbers, and names.

17. But substantive memories, the good memories that nourish and sustain us, give me a sense of history—my history with and without God. When I recall that God communicates with me, I remember the difference accepting Christ made in my life.

18. How else can we deal with the hurts of our past except through our memories? Robert Wood developed the Living Reminder Retreat as an Upper Room spiritual formation program for local churches, utilizing *The Living Reminder* by Henri Nouwen. In

the Living Reminder Retreat, we study the three types of memory Professor Nouwen describes—healing, guiding, and sustaining memories. Participants are most keenly interested in healing memories because many of them have memories of negative experiences that have never been healed. Usually they have shunned or repressed their memories. But healing doesn't work like that. Nothing is ever gained by pretending that a thing did not happen.

19. Professor Nouwen talks about "celebrating our hurts." For most, that is a new thought. "What is there to celebrate? I want to forget the hurt and move on." But celebrating one's hurt is just the point. We celebrate a hurt by giving it prominence again in the memory—by uncovering it and looking at it. Then we are able to deal with it. The hurt has no power over us; only the memory of it has power. When the hurt is remembered and offered to God, the hurt can be healed.

20. God communicates with us through our good memories when they put us in touch again with the care and providence and grace of God. God also communicates with us through our bad memories when we place them into divine care and grace.

Will

21. The human will is also a port of entry that God uses to communicate with us, and it is probably the easiest of the five to understand. We all have experienced either the presence or absence of strength of will. Fr. Powell describes alcoholics who find strength in their will to do something that in themselves they were not previously able to do.

22. During a week when I paid special attention to persons around me, I witnessed dramatic effects of God's communicating through the will:

- A blind woman in her mid-twenties received her college diploma.
- Someone sitting behind me commented as a man walked forward to get his college diploma, "That man with a wooden leg is my fifty-seven-year-old daddy."
- "I don't want to put the tests off. Whatever is wrong, we need to know so it can be treated."
- "I want to set the record straight. I have been unfaithful in my marriage."

• "I love my car and I hate like everything to give it up, but I know it is only right that I do."

In each case, strength of will made the difference.

23. We know that God has communicated with us when we do that which in our natural strength we would not be prone to do or able to do.

Mind

24. The mind is one of the strongest things we have going for us in spiritual discernment. To be able to think and reason is to use logic, assemble and assimilate data, make choices, and act out what "comes to mind." None of these is a contradiction or violation of spiritual discernment. On the contrary, we could not properly discern without our mental faculties.

25. God's ways, for the most part, are not shrouded in mystery. They are usually reasonable, logical, simple, and obvious. When I read the commandment, "Thou shall not kill," I can grasp it with my mind. I can see the logic in it. Our world is full of innumerable examples that are far less dramatic. When I want to know God's will on such matters, I simply use my mind. Because my mind, when under the control of the Holy Spirit, is a reliable discerner of God's will, I don't need a theology book or a prayer group to help me discern whether God wants me to abuse drugs.

26. Usually at some point during a discussion of the five ports of entry someone will question whether the list of five is complete. "How about Scripture or the witness of a Christian friend?" they will ask. "Doesn't God speak to us in those ways?"

27. I try to distinguish clearly between a source of witness and our perception of that witness. Our perception involves a port of entry. The Bible is a source of God's witness, to be sure. But how long does the Bible sit on the table, unopened and unread? It is the same with the Christian witness of a friend. That witness may have been effectively given in word and deed on numerous occasions, yet it can remain unheeded—never really heard! Only when one makes use of the Bible or the Christian witness does it move through a port of entry into one's consciousness.

The Body

28. A professor friend of mine described a personal experience that strongly suggests that our bodies may be channels through which God communicates with us. This professor was successful and found affirmation in his work at the university. He was teaching effectively and receiving a wonderful response from his students. The university moved him into a coveted tenured faculty position within six months, when for others it took five years. His ample salary also affirmed the quality of his work. Everything was great, except that every morning when he went to work he became nauseated—really sick. A medical checkup discovered nothing wrong. After nine months of daily nausea at work, his wife said, "Is it possible that God is trying to speak to you through your body and you are not listening? Maybe this is not what you are supposed to be doing with your life."

29. In due time, my friend left the university and began a year's sabbatical in residence with his family at Pendle Hill, the Quaker Retreat Center near Philadelphia. He stayed at Pendle Hill as a leader for ten more years at a sizable reduction in salary. And he never again experienced daily nausea.

30. To be serious about discerning God's will, two basic understandings must be deeply fixed in one's life of prayer and personal theology. First, God is good! If you do not hold that basic conviction, why would you want to know God's will? The other foundation belief is just as simple: *Communication with God is possible.*

> If you wish intentionally to develop your capactiy for discerning God's will, the best way is to open and utilize all the ports of entry that are available to God for communicating with you!

31. We have considered the question of *how* God communicates with us. Now let's make it a purely quantitative question. Let's not ask *how* but *how much*—or *how little*—God communicates with us. We can never determine this for sure, but we can surmise some things because of what we know about the nature of God. We know that God's grace is given freely and abundantly. We always experience weather, air, and the seasons. These simple reminders suggest that we need never have to question God's constancy.

32. God does not always have to be "speaking" or "broadcasting" in order to be communicating. Nor is communication from God stopped if I am not attentive. The very possibility of our presence to each other is the beginning of communication. And God is constantly calling for the full realization of that possibility. God's constancy in relationship—even constancy in *availability* for relationship—is in itself a powerful form of communication. In a deep, deep sense, that communication goes on all the time. It is like my relationship with Rosalie. We have a deep relationship of communication in part because of our *availability* for a deep relationship.

33. How *much* God communicates with me is a wonderful question that opens up marvelous images of totality and constancy that reflect God's nature. How *little* I communicate with God is a terrible question because it confronts me precisely at the point of one of my weaknesses. The answer to that question judges me for my inability to receive what God is saying because I refuse to have "ears to hear." The major factor determining how little I communicate with God is the closed or underdeveloped ports of entry to my consciousness. Considering such a gift, how little I communicate with God is a matter of everlasting *disgrace* on my part. How *much* God communicates with me by being constantly available to me is a matter of everlasting *grace* on God's part.

The Human Side of Spiritual Discernment, Continued

Day 1: Imagination

READING

Read about *imagination*, pages 71–72.

REFLECTION AND RECORDING

Think of your imagination:

IS YOUR STORY ANYTHING LIKE MY STORY, WHICH I DESCRIBED IN THE SECTION ON IMAGINATION?

If so, in the space below write your own personal account of how others tried to squelch your gift of imagination.

_____

_____

In your closing silence, offer your story of brokenness (squelched imagination) to God. Go in peace.

Day 2: Memory

READING

Read about *memory*, pages 72–73.

REFLECTING AND RECORDING

Have you considered that God communicates with you through your memory? God may want to communicate with you right now about a hurt in your life. If you wish to explore the possibility of "celebrating" a hurt, remember a hurt in your life that needs to be healed. To help you be specific, write it here (perhaps using a code you invent).

Once you have called the hurt forth by naming it—and by writing it—you need to find the best way to respond to it. Usually the recalling of a hurt brings its own instructions: It may call for confession, talking with a friend, or a deliberate act of forgiveness of one or more persons.

If your hurt involves a person who is now deceased, your response may be all the more urgent, although not easier. Do what you can do. Perhaps a special friend will be most helpful here. Talk it through by saying to the friend what you wish you had said to the person. Seek the understanding of your friend as though he or she is proxy for the other. Go as far as you can and do all you can to make it right, and then pray that by God's grace it will be right.

By remembering a hurt, you will be able to deal positively with it. You can never deal with it if it remains to fester under the surface.

Read again paragraph 19, page 73. Now it is up to you to care for your hurt in the way you have chosen.

Day 3: Will

READING

Read about *will*, pages 73–74.
Read Philippians 2:13.

REFLECTION AND RESPONSE

First, read again the list of examples of strength in the will on page 73.

Next, make a list of persons you know who have recently demonstrated strong will:

_____

_____

_____

_____

_____

Write the verse from Philippians 2:13:

_____

_____

How about strength of will in your own life? Describe a personal example of how this Scripture has been true for you.

Do you need for God to " . . . work in you to will and to act according to *God's* good purpose"? Name the specific area where you need strength to act:

_____

In a time of prayer, ask God to put strength in your will at that point of need in your life.

Day 4: Mind

READING

Read about *Mind* on page 74.

REFLECTION AND RESPONSE

1) Have you thought of your mind as a primary or secondary factor in your discernment of God's will?
Primary _____ Secondary _____
2) When you go to work, do you function primarily as:
Mind _____ Spirit _____ ?
3) When you go to church, do you function primarily as:
Mind _____ Spirit _____ ?

Below are two words—*mind* and *spirit*—with lines beneath each word. Beside the lines are two columns of words. Write each word you choose under the appropriate heading you think fitting, and try to pair words in the first column with those in the other column.

MIND	SPIRIT		
_____	_____	FEELING	LOGIC
_____	_____	THINK	FAITH
_____	_____	MYTHS	FACTS
_____	_____	BUSINESS	REALITY
_____	_____	SYMBOLISM	REASON
_____	_____	RELIGION	EMOTION

Draw a circle around the column of words under *mind* and

another around the column of words under *spirit* so that visually the columns are separated.

You have separated the columns with circles. Have you also separated them in your daily life? Consider that question carefully and then write your answer here (Yes or No): _____

Before you proceed, draw a large circle to enclose both columns. That is the way they were meant to be. That is the total you, and your mind is involved in every one of the items mentioned.

Review your answers to the three numbered questions and the exercise with the word columns above. Reflect upon the importance of your mind in your spirituality. After you pray, write your thoughts here: _____

_____

_____

Day 5: Body

READING

Read about *body*, pages 74–75.
Read Romans 12:1

REFLECTING AND RESPONDING

Write out Romans 12:1:

Notice the close relationship of the body with spiritual worship. Notice also the phrase, "bodies as living sacrifices." What is the difference between that phrase and "sacrificing your bodies" as in not caring for them or not listening to them? _____

_____

_____

Your body is a part of the real you to whom God communicates. Consider also that your body *communicates* with you?

What is your body saying (or trying to say to you) about your relationship with God? As you consider this question, let your writing grow out of your silence. _____

_____

_____

_____

Day 6: Your Church and the Ports of Entry

READING

Reread the major headings in Narrative Four and quickly
review the descriptions of the six ports of entry through which God
communicates with us.

REFLECTING AND RESPONDING

What are the implications for your church? How can more
people be made aware of these ports of entry? Write your thoughts
here:

_____

_____

What does this suggest you should *do*? _____
*As you prepare for tomorrow's workbook exercise, schedule
adequate time to complete the session before you go to church. Be
seated in the sanctuary a few minutes early so you will have some
quality silence to center on worship.*

Day 7: Communication: How Much or How Little?

It is important that you complete today's exercise before you go
to church today.

READING

Read paragraphs 32–33, pages 75–76.
Read 1 Corinthians 12:12–31.
Here are some key phrases from Narrative Four:
• God is good! Communication with God is possible.
• How *much* God communicates. How *little* God comunicates.
• God is always available for relationship.
• Everlasting *disgrace* on my part. Everlasting *grace* on God's
  part.
As you watch people come into church today, try to make a
connection between the Scripture reading, the narrative reading, and
your congregation. Think about this during the worship service
today, and take two or three minutes after the benediction to write
your thoughts on the lines below. *As you worship today, be praying
for members of your congregation.*

_____

As you go today, remember that God is constantly

Communicating to you, to the people in your church, and to *everyone*.

How *much* God communicates is a matter of everlasting *grace* on God's part!

Group Meeting Following Week Four

The leader will plan the meeting to last no more than an hour and a half, arrange chairs in a circle, and welcome participants. Start on time.

FIRST:
- Invite participants to review their workbooks and select one or more of the following points to talk about:
- The day of the week that was most meaningful.
- Something significant learned during the week.
- A question for the group to discuss now.
- A particular Scripture that needs to be discussed.
- A personal experience of imagination.
- Who has had the experience of "celebrating a hurt"?

How God Communicates

- Ask participants to select a port of entry to discuss from their own experience of either using it or neglecting it. (Make sure all ports of entry are discussed.)
- How is this congregation interpreting God's will?
- Any unusual or out-of-the-blue discernments?

How Was It in Church on Day Seven?

- Was it different from the previous Sunday?
- What did you learn from the Scripture reading?
- As a group, take two to three minutes of silence to consider this question: *When you think of the human side of spiritual discernment and then think of the people you saw in church on Day Seven, are you encouraged or discouraged about the possibility of God's being heard and seen (discerned) within your body of Christ?*
- After the silence: Discuss this question as a group.

How Shall Your Group Pray?

PRAYERS OF THANKSGIVING

Be thankful for evidence of the spiritual sensitivity and intentional faith journeys of your people.

PRAYERS OF INTERCESSION

Your group may choose prayers of intercession or petition for a new spiritual sensitivity within the body of Christ.

PRAYERS FOR GUIDANCE

Each of you and your group (and perhaps other persons and groups in your church) are being called to give strong leadership to help make your church capable of spiritual discernment. The ability to pray for guidance and to be open to receive guidance are two great gifts each of you has to give.

If your group can readily agree on how to pray, end your meeting with group prayer. If there is not easy consensus, select one of the following ways to close your meeting:

1) Each person prays silently and/or aloud in the particular way he or she chooses, or 2) divide into smaller groups to pray for thanksgiving, intercession, or guidance.

Whichever way you decide to spend your prayer time, come together as a group and end the meeting by praying the Lord's Prayer.

When the Power Comes

1. More than 300 times the New Testament mentions the word *power* as an expression of the Holy Spirit. Power. This word is translated from the Greek word *dunamis*, from which we get *dynamite*. So some 300 times the New Testament talks about dynamite coming to earth from heaven. This is an expression of the power of the Holy Spirit that is loose within and among and upon the people of God.

2. There are times when the unmistakable power of the Holy Spirit comes. Although direct spiritual revelation has come to me infrequently, I have had one experience of revelation that was unmistakably clear. I had nothing to discern; all I had to do was act. I want to describe that experience because the result of that gift of grace potentially affects all of us and our churches. First, here is my wife's account of part of this experience, which set the stage for what was to come.

ROSALIE

3. Danny called one morning and said, "I am getting ready to catch a plane. We have had a most unusual situation develop at The Upper Room. I don't want to worry you about this, but one of our staff persons put a little note on the bottom of a letter inviting people to send prayer requests to The Upper Room. He mailed the letter to about 20,000 people. It was a wonderful thought, but we are not prepared for what has happened. Two or three days ago we received 45 or 50 letters. Some of the letters contain donations and some are for orders for materials. Many of them also contain prayer requests. The next day we received nearly 250; the next day almost 500. We now have several baskets full of letters and have four secretaries at work on the mail. They are frantic. We don't know what to do. Rosalie, do anything within *reason*! I have to go, they are calling my plane."

4. I went into the family room where I had been reading the

Bible. I thought, "Lord, what a terrible mistake—but what a wonderful surprise. We've been needing a place to receive prayer requests like this all along, but what are we going to do?" I decided to call two friends in my prayer group. "I want each of you you to pray about this, and at 11:00 call back with your idea of what we ought to do."

5. All three of us had the same answer: Go to The Upper Room office and begin praying about the letters. The four secretaries had opened and sorted and piled mail everywhere. They were so frustrated that the last thing they could do was pray.

6. We each took a batch from the 2500 letters stacked in baskets all over two offices, and went to the Alone With God Chapel where for the next four hours we prayed together, read requests aloud, prayed separately, prayed looking out of the window, kneeling at the altar, sitting in the pews. We prayed on our knees; we held hands and prayed. We tried every method and position and combination that we could imagine. When we stopped to count, we had gone through only seventy-five prayer requests. We looked at each other and one of my friends said, "It is getting late. I am hungry and tired. What is our next step?"

7. The other said, "Let's go back to the Bible." We opened it and read this passage: "Again, I tell you that if two of you on earth agree about anything you ask for, it will be done for you by my Father in heaven. For where two or three come together in my name, there am I with them" (Matt. 18:19–20, NIV).

8. One of us said a brief prayer during which she led us symbolically to bring all the letters that we had with us and pile them on top of the Bible. We knelt at the altar while she prayed something like this, "Lord, we ask you to answer every need that is brought in these letters. We ask you to answer every need in all the letters that are downstairs in those offices. We ask you to answer every need that will ever come into this building. Help us know how to take care of the prayer needs of the world. Amen."

9. We gathered our letters, and with great joy realized that our work had been completed. We went back to the office and told the frustrated secretaries, "We've taken care of everything!" We were laughing. They were tired and puzzled. "What we have been praying about has been cared for," we explained. In the parking lot, someone said, "One day we will know what today has meant. We can know that because of this simple act of faith, something has been released in heaven that is very much needed."

10. When I recall this now, it is clear that we just took the next

step. That is all that God required of us—just to take the next step that was before us. We were not great pray-ers. We were three people who were not *trained* in anything. Our choice was to obey God with an openness to new approaches.

11. The design for the Living Prayer Center of The Upper Room came just a few weeks after that frustrating and wonderful day. Now the Living Prayer Center receives over 6000 prayer requests each month and is staffed with 125 volunteers.

*   *   *

DANNY

12. A number of weeks later, and seemingly totally unrelated to this story, Maxie Dunnam issued his final invitation to me to become Director of Prayer Life for The Upper Room. At that time he was World Editor and thus head of all Upper Room ministries. I was a staff member in the Evangelism Section of our Board of Discipleship.

13. I had great misgivings about accepting this new position and had refused it for a number of months. I did not see myself in that way. Each time I refused the new job we would talk about it, and I would feel both attracted and repelled by it. I felt desolation and consolation mixed together and I couldn't sort it out. One day Maxie said that he needed my final answer, that he couldn't wait any longer.

14. I spent a fitful weekend, caught between both positions. A lot of ego was mixed up in my response to that invitation. If you were invited to head up the prayer life movement of an entire denomination, how would you feel? But along with my ego were a lot of misgivings about how I would function in that position. I was not eager to jump into something I could not figure out how to handle.

15. All weekend I prayed earnestly, but I could not get any clarity in discernment. Finally, it was late Sunday afternoon. I went to our bedroom and shut the door so I would be away from everyone. I told God I wanted an answer: "God, I am tired of being raked across the cutting edge of indecision and I want to know for sure what I am supposed to do or not do. This straddling the fence is eating me alive. I want to know your will now!"

16. I was standing at the foot of our king-size bed with my back to it. Suddenly I stretched out my arms to the side and said, "God, give me a sign, one way or another." Then I took "the Nestea plunge." I fell back into the middle of the bed as a symbol of total surrender. I wanted desperately to know the will of God. I lay there

for a moment with my eyes closed, face up on the bed. Suddenly, the room began to spin. I suppose I experienced vertigo. It was frightening! My heart began to race at an alarming rate. Everything in the world was topsy-turvy and moving and spinning.

17. It didn't take much of that to shake me up. I opened my eyes and was amazed to find everything was in place—the dresser, the chair, the room. I lay there for a moment and looked around. But I seemed to be all right. Nothing broken. My heart was still racing but at least it was working. I wondered whether the same thing might happen again. I closed my eyes and the intensity of the sensation was greater than before. I was determined to endure it longer, but the vertigo increased so much that I grabbed the bed to keep from falling off, even though I was lying in the middle. When I opened my eyes, everything was back in order.

18. After I began to breathe normally, I said, "Lord, are you trying to tell me something? Are you giving me a sign?" Suddenly it dawned on me. "If I were to accept this invitation, are you telling me that there would be nothing but confusion and turmoil and chaos? Is that what would result?"

19. Something inside of me died on that bed that day. I gave it up—all the ego along with all the anxiety. "Thank you for lifting this burden," I prayed.

20. At dinner, I said to Rosalie, "Dear, I've decided that we are not going to The Upper Room."

21. "Oh? Have some potatoes."

22. It was all right. It was OK. A decision had been made and that was good. It was a good decision because even potatoes had suddenly become more important. I didn't think another thing about the job offer. The issue was gone . . . over . . . settled.

23. I woke on Monday morning with a vibrant spiritual sensitivity, such as I had never had before or since—except for the following day. It was marvelous. It was an ecstatic feeling. I felt a surge of strength and power coming into me, flooding my consciousness. I drove to work on cloud nine. While I worked on the usual, natural plane, my mind and my spirit soared. It was an indescribably wonderful, creative day. I didn't tell anyone that I was living in another world as I functioned routinely. I had such a deep sense of joy within me. Insights and conclusions and images were coming into my mind and everything seemed to fit so beautifully.

24. I went to bed that night with no fear that such a wonderful day would end and, with it, the inspiration that had made it special. Sure enough, when I awoke the next morning, I felt a continuation at the same intensity. All through that Tuesday the same exhilarating insights continued. Everything was falling into place. All of my ideas about how a prayer ministry could be shaped had died, gone. Now there was a clean slate, and God was writing upon my imagination what might be. It was beautiful. It was inspired.

25. On the morning that Maxie said, "I have to have your decision today," I began to describe for him the inspiration that had come in that two-day period: A Living Prayer Center . . . Covenant Prayer Groups all across the country that take seriously the ministry of intercessory prayer. The groups would be schooled in prayer to help them become responsible intercessors. What if Covenant Prayer Groups met regularly and were linked together through the telephone by volunteers in the Prayer Center? Why not have an Upper Room Prayer Meeting once a month, where we bring the finest people in prayer we can find from all over the world, record their sessions and make two thirty-minute teaching tapes? We could then give the tapes without charge to the Covenant Prayer Groups across the country to keep them on the growing edge of their own personal life of prayer. What would happen if . . . and I described the newsletter for Covenant Groups and a philosophy of funding to ensure that we would not ask for money from people who called for prayer. I described all the pieces of the gift of insight that had been given during those two grace-filled days.

26. Maxie said, "I perceive that I have your answer." My reply surprised me almost as much as it surprised him. I had immediately realized that what he said was true. Across those two days of intense spiritual insight about the concepts and guidelines for a prayer ministry, I had had no thoughts about "selling" these ideas to Maxie, just the wonder and fascination of sharing them with him. I had simply received and held them in the white light of gratitude. This was the plan and both of us had seen it. The spiritual gift of those two days had been recognized and confirmed by a spiritual friend—and therein was a call to ministry for The Upper Room and for me.

27. Perhaps it was through the experience of being underprepared to respond adequately to the prayer needs of people, coupled with the spiritual gift of guidance about how to respond, that The Upper Room Prayer Ministry was born. Now I see that the spiritual discernment process was fully operative during the months of wrestling with such a great unmet need.

28. The Nestea plunge was an experience of death and resurrection. Old plans and ideas died so that new insights could be born. In watching the marvelous rhythm of how God interacts with us, I find that death and resurrection are a major theme in our spiritual journey. We have to die (or something in us has to die) in order for something to be born. Isn't that how the power comes?

29. "Stay here in the city until you have been clothed with power from on high" (Luke 24:49, NRSV). In that tarrying, there will likely be a need for dying. We must get to the place through our own death to self where we can say, "God's will *only*." Death and resurrection! They are unmistakably at the heart of the Christian faith, and I suspect that they are at the heart of spiritual discernment.

Introduction To Week Five and Week Six Exercises
Spiritual Discernment as a Gift of God to the People

Welcome to Week Five and Week Six of your workbook of spiritual discernment. The content of the workbook pages in these two weeks will provide a bridge from personal to corporate discernment.

The gift of discernment is not something we possess so much as it is a gift that God eagerly gives to everyone who earnestly wants to know God's will. Obedience, surrender, and death and resurrection (which we shall consider on the first three days) are key factors, but they are not mutually exclusive. They are interwoven and complement each other. When they reside within you, they help prepare you to receive the gift God wants to give to you and to all God's people—the gift of discernment.

Narrative Five moves beyond the human elements that we considered last week to three major components of obedience, surrender, and death and resurrection. When operative, these prepare the way for discernment.

In Narrative Six, we cross the bridge into corporate discernment and the importance (and difficulty) of consensus. On days four, five, and six, you will be guided to develop a plan to introduce and advocate spiritual discernment in a group that is important to you.

On day seven, you will explore a new view of your congregation as a place where spiritual discernment is—or is meant to be—a way of life.

The overriding questions during these two weeks are:
What will you do with God's gift of discernment?
What will your church do with it?

Spiritual Discernment as a Gift of God to the People

Day 1: Obedience in Spiritual Discernment

READING

> Read Narrative Five, *When the Power Comes*.
> Read Exodus 3:1–4:20.

REFLECTION AND RESPONSE

Last week we considered the human elements involved in spiritual discernment. This week we look at discernment as God's gift, which is given to all who are ready to receive it.

Narrative Five described three major components in this experience of discernment about The Upper Room Prayer Ministry: obedience, surrender, and death and resurrection. These may be common components to help prepare us to receive God's gift of discernment, so let's consider each of the three on successive days as we begin this week.

Today we will examine obedience as a component of discernment. Rosalie reported that she and her friends prayed about the problem of the bulging baskets of mail and came up with the same answer: "Go to the office and pray about the letters." Seventy-five prayer requests and four hours later, they felt that their task had been completed. One of them said, "One day we will know what today has meant. We can know that something great has happened this day. Because of this simple act of faith, something has been released in heaven that is very much needed."

Rosalie's summary expressed the strategic role that obedience had played: "We just took the next step. That is all that God required of us. We were not great pray-ers. We were three people who were not specially trained. Our choice was to be obedient and open to searching for God's answer." Obedience in taking the next step probably a key to discernment for you!

To be *obedient to God* in your personal question/issue of which

92

you wrote most recently on Week 2/Day 5, what steps do you need to take next? List them here:

Remember, obedience is a key component of spiritual discernment.

Day 2: Surrender as a Key Component in Spiritual Discernment

READING

Read paragraphs 15–19, pages 87–88.

REFLECTION AND RESPONSE

"God, I want to know your will!" When I surrendered on my bed that day, I did not know I was using a key to discernment. It felt more like an act of desperation. But surrender to God is a key component of discernment! Are you ready for surrender?

Is the question/issue you face important to you?
Yes ____ No ____
Have you considered surrendering yourself to God?
Yes ____ No ____
Are you willing to surrender to God now?
Yes ____ No ____

If your answers are yes, write your prayer of surrender here:

_____

_____

_____

_____

If you answered no to one of the questions above, reflect on it in silence and answer:

What does this say about me?

_____

_____

_____

Day 3: Look at Zacchaeus

READING

Read Luke 19:1–10.

REFLECTION AND RESPONSE

How did Zacchaeus experience surrender? _____

_____

_____

What does Zacchaeus' story teach you? _____

_____

_____

Day 4: Death and Resurrection in Spiritual Discernment

READING

Read John 12:20–26.

REFLECTION AND RESPONSE

On Day One we considered *obedience*. On Days Two and Three, *surrender*. Today, *death and resurrection*.

In Narrative Five I wrote, "The Nestea plunge was an experience of death and resurrection for me. Old plans and ideas died so that new insights could be born. I have been watching the marvelous rhythm of how God interacts with us and I find that death and resurrection are a major theme in our spiritual journey. We have to die (or something in us has to die) in order for something to be born. Isn't that how the power comes?" I am now even more convinced that this is true! My guess is that if I ask you to write in your workbook something in you that needs to die, it would be very difficult for you to do so. But give it a try.

_____

It is more probable that you will have to work your way—or pray your way—to recognition of it. Dying to self is not only important but common in spiritual discernment. You may need to surrender your old ideas or previous plans. I did. They were blocking me from discerning God's will.

Try to work your way to face something honestly—anything—
that is blocking your discernment of God's will. Or better still, see
whether you can *pray* your way to it. Read the passage from John
again as preparation for silence. Pay close attention to verse 24:
"Truly, truly, I say to you, unless a grain of wheat falls into the earth
and dies, it remains alone; but if it dies, it bears much fruit."

In eight to ten minutes of silence, ask the Holy Spirit to bring to
your mind anything to which you need to die. Is something blocking
you from knowing God's will? Pray and wait in silence. Write any
thoughts, ideas, or words that come to you in the silence.

Review what you have just written. What do you need to do
about it? Write your thoughts here:

_____

_____

Answer this question: *Am I ready for something [be specific] to
die in me so something can be born?*
What is it? _____

Day 5: Defining Consensus in Corporate Discernment

READING

Read Narrative Six, *The Higher Way of Spiritual Discernment.*
Read Acts 15:1–22

REFLECTION AND RESPONSE

As we turn to Narrative Six, we begin to consider God's gift of
discernment from the corporate—rather than the personal or individual—perspective. When persons corporately try to discern God's
will, *consensus* becomes a necessary factor.

On days five and six of this week we examine two experiences
of consensus and formulate a plan to experiment with the principle of
consensus in corporate discernment. Focus on a group in which you
participate to serve as a frame of reference in which to apply the
principles of consensus in corporate discernment.

Write on the line below a setting where spiritual discernment is
needed: your family, church, Sunday school class, organization,
business, etc. Be specific and write your selection here: _____

Day 6: Why Consensus?

READING

Read paragraphs 9–15, pages 105–6.
Read Acts 15:23–30.

REFLECTION AND RESPONSE

Are you part of a group within the church that might be open to making decisions by consensus? Think about it and list no more than three of the groups in which you participate.

( ) _____

( ) _____

( ) _____

Now put a check mark by the one—or more than one—that you think may be open to decision making by consensus. Below list some of the matters in that group that need spiritual discernment:

Note here how you might begin to introduce the concept of spiritual discernment by consensus. Consensus does not mean regimentation nor beating down the opposition nor everyone having to give in to everyone else. List persons you would talk to about it and when.

As you prepare for tomorrow's workbook exercise, schedule adequate time to complete the session before you go to church. Be seated in the sanctuary a few minutes early so you will have some quality silence to focus on worship.

Day 7: Looking for Living Examples

> **Note:** It is important that you complete today's exercise before you go to church today.

READING

Read again 1 Corinthians 12:12–31.

REFLECTION AND RESPONSE

This is your fifth Sunday to read this passage as you think of your church—a place where the body of Christ becomes visible.

Note any persons who are examples of obedience and/or surrender, or who have experienced the powerful rhythm of death and resurrection. Put their initials on the line (before the slash) by the appropriate experience.

_____ / _____ Obedience

_____ / _____ Surrender

_____ / _____ Death and resurrection

How about yourself? Do the same with your initials.

In a time of prayer, thank God for the witness of these persons and for the witness of your own life. *Return to your notebook after church so you can fill in the blanks in this exercise.*

Group Meeting Following Week Five

The leader will plan the meeting to last no more than an hour and a half, arrange chairs in a circle, and welcome participants. Start on time.

FIRST: Invite participants to review their workbooks and select one or more of the following points to talk about:
- The day of the week that was most meaningful
- A significant learning of the week
- A question for the group to discuss now

NEXT: During Weeks Three and Four and at our last meeting, we thought about the human side of discernment. At this meeting we will turn the coin and look at *God's gift* of discernment to the people.

It is appropriate to begin with a pivotal Scripture passage. Instead of using the following Scripture for personal use during Week 5, it was saved until now so that we could consider it together.

NEXT: Read aloud in the group 1 Corinthians 12:4–11.

In verse 10, Paul described one gift as "the ability to distinguish between spirits." This is commonly referred to as the gift of discernment and usually connotes discernment *of* spirits or discernment *between or among* spirits.

The significance of the gift of discernment is not in the person who has received it but what he or she does with it and how that person responds to God because of it. This gift, like all the others given by the Holy Spirit, is given for ministry to build up the body of Christ. It is not a badge; it is not reserved for the spiritually elite; it is seldom (if ever) permanently bestowed upon a person.

The gift of discernment is a gift of God for the people. If you are given the gift of discernment for a moment or longer, receive it and use it freely. It is not something you have whipped up, and it does not make you spiritually superior. It is a gift to be used for your own good and the good of others.

We have talked about discernment as a gift for *everyone*. But it is not constant. You may minister with the gift of discernment today and be ministered to by someone else through the gift of discernment tomorrow. That is part of the strength of the body of Christ.

To say that discernment is a gift of God in no way repudiates the importance of practicing the principles of discernment. Through such use we become more aware of how God is known to us and how we can respond to God. God more eagerly gives the gift of discernment to persons who prepare themselves to receive it.

In silence let's take a few minutes to read 1 Corinthians 12:4–11 and to reflect upon its meaning and reality for us.

There may be a desire for discussion after the silence.

*   *   *

Last week we looked at obedience, surrender, and death and resurrection. Ask each person to tell which of those three categories has most nearly touched his or her experience. Have participants divide themselves into small groups.

Take eight to ten minutes for group members to talk about their experiences with obedience, surrender, or death and resurrection, emphasizing the strength or weakness of the experience.

Closing Prayer Time

As you prepare to end the meeting, read the following suggestions and sit quietly in your circle in silence:

1) Think about the *living examples* of spirituality in your church.

2) Think about particular persons in the other groups using this workbook (if any), for they will be your allies.

3) Think about the group to which you plan to speak about spiritual discernment by consensus.

During a verbal prayer, the leader will name each of the groups mentioned in numbers 1, 2, and 3 above, allowing time after each category for persons to call out names that come to mind. This naming is a prayer:
 • a prayer of thanksgiving for the person named;
 • a prayer of intercession for that person;
 • a prayer of petition for the church.
By praying for our people and our church this way, we will be giving prayer support to the efforts we will make.

When you begin this experience of prayer, the leader will call for (1) names of living examples of spirituality in our church (pause for names to be given); (2) names of persons in the other groups (pause for names to be given); and (3) the groups that you will speaking to (pause for the naming of groups). Pray for persons or concerns known to the group. Close with The Lord's Prayer.

Corporate Discernment

The Challenge of Consensus

"Let me interrupt this program to bring you a special announcement . . . "

We have reached the end of the section on personal discernment. We now make a transition to the final three narratives and the workbook weeks that cover corporate discernment.

Corporate discernment is the other side of the coin of personal discernment. A significant mental shift will be necessary. You have been thinking about your own personal discernment. During the next three weeks you will think corporately—about others and how you can challenge them with a new way to be and to do.

It may help if you consider that until now you have been doing this study for yourself. Now you are to continue for the sake of others. The next three weeks can be just as rewarding as the preceding five weeks if everyone understands that although corporate discernment is not so easy to experience as personal discernment, it is essential for the body of Christ.

So, as a group, consciously make this needed transition. Close your eyes . . . take a deep breath . . . and offer your own silent prayer . . . that this next part will actually be the best and most significant part because you are doing it for your sisters and brothers in Christ!

When you are ready to proceed be sure to read again the **Introduction to Week Five and Week Six** *on page 91 before continuing with Narrative Six and Week Six.*

The Higher Way of Spiritual Discernment

1. The process of developing the Academy for Spiritual Formation had been underway for almost five years. It began to take shape in fragmentary ways during my four-month sabbatical in 1978, when I had searched for a place to study spirituality. I wanted to begin a focused study of Christian spirituality that would be historically comprehensive and experientially helpful. I could not find a Protestant setting for this endeavor other than a seminary.

2. Maxie Dunnam and I had discussed a great unmet need— significant training in Christian spirituality for the many people who were eager for something more than what was then available. Those long discussions were interesting but frustrating because an answer seemed beyond our grasp. But our conversations were also highly productive. Though we did not realize it at the time, intense spiritual discernment occurred as we talked. To wrestle with an issue that is greater than you are, and to clarify the need, prepares you to discern a direction for a suitable response. We agreed that since I was ready for a "deeper plunge" I should spend my four-month study leave in a setting where I could begin a new dimension of my spiritual journey. The timing seemed to be right.

3. Over several months I looked at many places and inquired of many people. One evening I called Dr. Morton Kelsey. I knew him only through his writings on prayer and spirituality. Dr. Kelsey's words confirmed what others had hinted. He said, "I am sorry to say that you can't find what you are looking for anywhere in this country." He then suggested I find a spiritual guide who could help me put together a program of study, visit a variety of centers, and reflect on Christian spirituality.

4. Gradually, a rough plan for the Academy For Spiritual Formation began to emerge. The plan was formed out of experiences, conversations, readings, and hunches gathered from here and there. My visits gave me a broad sampling of expressions of spirituality: Roman Catholic monasteries and houses of prayer, renewal centers, camp meetings, Bible courses, parachurch institutions, and eight or ten varied denominational expressions of spirituality.

5. At last, I wrote the basic model for the Academy For Spiritual Formation, a spirituality program to which people would make a two-year commitment. They would meet together for five days each calendar quarter. The rationale for the Academy was as follows:

> The Academy (a center for specialized learning and experience) recognizes that the Holy Spirit is the enabling power in all Christian spiritual formation. The Academy is designed to provide a setting for a spiritually disciplined community where lay and clergy can open their lives to receive God's love and grace to the end that they increasingly become spiritual leaven within the Body of Christ.

The Academy would have a holistic emphasis on body, mind, and spirit. It would offer emphases on physical fitness and nutrition (body), sixteen courses covering a broad spectrum of Christian spirituality (mind), and worship through daily prayer and spiritual disciplines (spirit).

6. Everything except the curriculum was coming together fairly well. I kept asking, "What would you teach fifty people who want to study spirituality over a two-year period?" Everyone I asked had a different answer. The right answer for the church, however, was important enough that I wanted to do whatever was necessary to find it.

7. I invited several people who were far along in their study and practice of Christian spirituality to form a consortium to put the final touches on the Academy model and to determine the curriculum. The group was theologically diverse. Six denominations (including Roman Catholic) were represented.

8. For a year and a half we worked to flesh out the model. Still curriculum development eluded us. So I called for a two-day meeting of the Advisory Board, a session that demanded careful planning. The group included about twenty high-powered people from a variety of theological positions and religious heritages, who were authorities on spirituality. I shuddered to think of all the ways we could get bogged down in semantics or sidetracked in theological confusion.

9. I hired a consultant and we decided that because the stakes were so high and the content under consideration was of such a special nature, we needed a different—a higher and better—way of making decisions than by voting an item up or down. The nature of our content suggested the method: *Spiritual discernment would be needed to deal adequately with spiritual matters.* That's it! We would interact on the basis of spiritual discernment. But what if some discern one thing and some another? Would we then be reduced to voting? No, there was one additional requirement: consensus!

10. Why consensus?

11. My question at the time was "why not consensus?" Here Christians were trying to discern the will of God on a matter that could profoundly affect the people of God. I was convinced of three things: (1) God's will for the Academy was so essential that we must do whatever it takes to know it. (2) God's will is not so multifaceted or diffused or cloudlike that it cannot be discerned. (3) God's will is revealed in our seeking, for God wants us to know and act upon the divine will far more than we are prone to do.

12. Therefore, I felt confident that if we came together and earnestly tried to know God's will, it could be known—and that we could all know it at once.

13. Our use of consensus would not be a litmus test nor a safeguard nor an effort to prove something. It would be a spiritual ingredient of our relationship. We would be committed to hear each other, learn from each other, and bring forth the best in each other. Consensus would not mean that the many would hold out or gang up on the few until they abandoned their position or came around to what a majority of the others wanted to do. It meant that God's will was so important to each person that nothing else mattered.

14. I thought of the image of a prism being turned until the light hits it just right. Some issues or questions would require little or no turning. But when an issue needed to be considered from many points of view, we would continue to turn it in the light until the truth was revealed. Then everyone could see it at once. The process of turning an issue might sometimes mean giving up something or adding to or modifying or replacing something altogether. At the meeting, consensus did not shackle our progress, for that meeting was one of the most productive any of us had ever attended. Consensus was our way of being with each other, and it had the same feel to it as the love we felt among us.

15. When I introduced this process to the Advisory Board, nods greeted the proposal. Spiritual discernment by consensus was indeed a higher and welcomed way. I suggested that if someone simply could not finally agree with a particular point, we would welcome a minority report. After all, we were not only interested in the best decision, but the best thinking on any subject. Spiritual energy charged the air, and creativity was the result. All spoke freely, strongly advocating positions. But we were united in earnestly seeking God's will on everything. We kept changing, shaping, and turning an issue until the light hit it just right. When it did, everyone could see it. It was amazing! By the end of our meeting no issues were unsettled. The task was completed on time, with consensus on every point. There was no need for a minority report. We went away feeling that we had been together in a new way—a higher way—on holy ground. Spiritual discernment by consensus! A new and remarkable way of being and doing.

*   *   *

16. This was not the only experience of spiritual discernment in the Academy. The procedure had worked so well for the Advisory Board that I suggested that the Leadership Team should make its final plans and lead the first Academy by consensus.

17. A remarkable experience of spiritual discernment by consensus occurred at the first meeting of the team. At the earlier consortium meeting the Advisory Board had developed guidelines for the curriculum, ending with a list of nine. That list was a major accomplishment of our two-day meeting. When we met as the Leadership Team, our task was to implement the guidelines and specify sixteen courses.

18. John was on the Leadership Team and present at the consortium meeting. As the Leadership Team began the process of identifying courses, John gave us a list he had drawn up. When we compared his list with the curriculum guidelines, we found an almost exact match. To our amazement, with the reversal of two courses, we had a perfect match! Then we reviewed our verbatim notes of the consortium meeting and we still had a match! After we determined that his list of courses matched the criteria set by the Advisory Board, John told us he had made the list of courses *before* the Advisory Board drew up the guidelines.

19. We sat in stunned silence, trying to absorb the meaning of what he had said! It took a while to comprehend what seemed like an example of "inverted discernment." All of us knew that John had not manipulated the guidelines to reflect his list of courses. He had been a member on the team just like everyone else. In helping to set the guidelines, he had not been more assertive or outspoken than the others. The fact that he had made his list of courses several weeks before the Advisory Board meeting made his list truly remarkable.

20. What I learned from this was equally remarkable. It confirmed a truth about spiritual discernment that sounds like a contradition: God's will is not fixed and unchanging, but it is definite and particular. That being true, I suppose it is inappropriate to think of inverted discernment. By whomever or whenever God's will for the Academy was discerned, God's will in that particular instance would be the same and could be known by all who discerned it.

21. Forty-seven participants plus two adjunct faculty persons at each session and six Leadership Team members were involved in the first Academy. For the first couple of sessions (five days each) we occasionally mentioned that the Leadership Team made decisions through spiritual discernment by consensus. We drew up this list of learnings, which we shared with Academy participants:

• Spiritual discernment by consensus takes time.

• The consensus process does not preclude an agenda.

• Some important matters do not need to be discerned, e.g., accepting a report, approval of minutes.

• Other matters can best be determined through discernment by consensus, e.g., is the idea we are considering the will of God?

• Death and resurrection are involved in the discernment process.

• The process calls for mutual vulnerability.

• Turfdom is sublimated. All persons involved must be committed to seek God's will even when it means giving up something.

• If there is no consensus, the previous decision stands or no decision is made.

• It is desirable to identify issues for discernment in advance to allow the group to consider them prayerfully.

• At the beginning of the discernment process each person assumes responsibility for his or her position rather than, "Well, a lot of people are saying. . . ." The adversarial style of debate is transformed into searching and complementary relationships.

• Listening to others takes on greater importance when you are trying to hear the voice of God speaking through them.

• When we gather for discernment, God is with us.

• Discernment by consensus involves testing a decision, i. e., what fruits does it produce?

22. Participants asked, "Why can't the church operate like this? In the church we make decisions by using *Robert's Rules of Order*— an adversarial model. It has the potential for polarizing people. As a result of the way most churches handle conflicting points of view, people are often divided and hard feelings are created. The adversarial model seems at times to be counterproductive to the purpose of the church because of what it does to people."

23. To what extent are the people of churches like yours and mine *actively* involved in discerning God's will? That becomes a critical question for all churches since every church has the responsibility, the calling—and the capacity—to be a spiritually discerning church. We all dream of a new and higher way to be the church. Many of us wish that our leaders would be capable discerners of God's will for the church so we can find ourselves and get on the move again. But we are "our leaders."

24. Since so much depends on how we shape the life of the congregation, equal attention must be given to how people discern God's will as they make decisions for the congregation. This suggests that a church practicing spiritual discernment principles will shape its communal life differently from a church that carries on "business as usual."

25. Therefore, in the next narrative we will consider: How is it possible for a local congregation to utilize spiritual discernment by consensus?

Getting Serious About Discernment

Day 1: Finalize Your Plan

READING

Review the reading you did and the notes you made on Day 6 of Week Five.

REFLECTION AND RESPONSE

How would you define consensus in discernment, and how would you introduce the concept to members of the group that you listed on Day 6?

Write your own definition of "discernment by consensus":

Think of the group you selected on Day 6 (or another group if a more appropriate one has come to mind) and write a statement to introduce the importance of consensus in corporate discernment. You may wish to outline specific points or write a full explanation in your own words. (Please use a separate piece of paper for this.)

Day 2: Why Consensus Is Possible in Spiritual Discernment

READING

Read paragraphs 16–20, pages 107–8.

REFLECTION AND RESPONSE

"God's will is not fixed and unchanging, but it is definite and particular."

Consensus is possible in discernment because God's will is definite and particular at any given moment!

Have you thought of God's will as definite and particular? Many people:

_____ think of God as begrudgingly secretive, and unexpressive, as mysteriously absent from human awareness.

_____ think that God shows partiality toward deeply spiritual people.

_____ think of God's will as hidden or elusive.

_____ have never seriously tried to discern God's will.

_____ have tried, but seldom, if ever, succeeded in discerning God's will.

Put a check mark by any of the above remarks that describe you.

Perhaps some in your selected group also hold negative attitudes about God and God's will. Would it be worthwhile to bring this subject to their attention?

- Is it important to you? Yes _____ No _____
- Would they benefit from such a discussion?
  Yes _____ No _____
- Are you willing to present it? Yes _____ No _____

Pray for your church and your selected group.

Day 3: If You Are Willing!

READING

Review what you wrote on Day 6 of last week.

REFLECTION AND RESPONSE

Consider doing the following:

1) With your group, share your concern to know God's will on the particular matter that you have in common.

2) Introduce spiritual discernment by consensus, using your workbook notes prepared on Day 6 of last week.

3) Discuss any of the negative attitudes about God or God's will that were considered yesterday within your selected group.

4) After affirming that *God's will is definite and particular*, and can be corporately discerned, ask your group to consider using the principles of corporate discernment.

Do not rush participants into a decision. If only a few in the group wish to participate, proceed with them.

Day 4: Why Consensus Is Difficult in Spiritual Discernment

READING

Read the "list of learnings" beginning on page 108.

REFLECTION AND RESPONSE

We must be realistic. Corporate discernment is not easy or quick. Consensus cannot be forced or rushed. Read the three preconditions for discernment, paragraph 9, pages 42f.

As you prepare your presentation to your selected group, those preconditions must be considered. *On the material you prepared on Day 6, make a note to include these in your presentation.*

Turn to the "list of learnings" on page 108 and put a check mark by points on the list that make consensus difficult. Because your selected group may also need to consider these as you invite members to practice the principles of corporate discernment, ask group them to discuss some of the points you have checked.

Reflect on what your church could be like if spiritual discernment were a way of life in your congregation. Don't think of your church as it is now—but of what it can become. Imagine a new church with a new way to *be* and a new way to *do*.

Pray about your church and the group you have been considering. After you have prayed, write your thoughts here:

Day 5: The Next Move Is Up to You

READING

Review the days of this week, beginning with Day 2.

REFLECTION AND RESPONSE

It is important for you to see this week's content as a whole, because the next move is up to you.

Here are three options:

1) Review and reflect upon this week's workbook pages and let your learnings continue to simmer in the hope that some day these principles of discernment can take root in you.
2) Decide now that you will continue to complete the plan you have been developing, and begin to cultivate an opening to discuss this with your selected group.
3) Complete your plan and introduce it now.

Which of the three options above do you choose? _____

Regardless of your choice, you and your church are ahead! Think of it:

- You have a developing vision of a great way to live!
- Since in your church others are probably using this workbook, a corporate vision is being developed.
- When you discern that the time is right, you and others will be prepared with a plan that is bold and practical.
- Proceed now; it is not a minute too soon!

Conclude your time today in silence to ask for guidance about what you should do and when you should do it.

Write your decision(s) here and go in peace.

What will I do? _____

When will I do it? _____

Day 6: Who Are You In This Plan?

READING

Read paragraph 23, page 109.

REFLECTION AND RESPONSE

Can you see your role in corporate spiritual discernment? Write a simple job description for someone like you who has the opportunity you have to lead your church in this method.

As you prepare for tomorrow's workbook exercise, schedule time to complete the exercise before you go to church. Be seated in the sanctuary a few minutes early so you will have a period of silence to center in for worship.

Day 7: Whom Do You Bring to Church With You?

Note: It is important that you complete today's workbook exercise before you go to church today.

READING

Read again 1 Corinthians 12:12–31.

REFLECTION AND RESPONSE

This is your sixth Sunday to read this passage as you prepare for church. What does it say to you that you didn't see when you first began to read it? How do you see your church differently now than when we began?

Now about the plan you have been developing these past few days: As you think about the people in your selected group and the people who will probably be in church with you today, remember that it is among these people (and some who cannot be present today) that your plan must work. Some are feet, some hands, some eyes, ears, noses.

> . . . God has so arranged the body . . . that there may be no dissension within the body; but the members may have the same care one for another (vv. 24–25, NRSV).

Your worshiping congregation is not the group with which to start your plan. You have selected a smaller group to introduce to the principles of consensus in corporate discernment. Then you developed and refined your plan so you can talk with your selected group about it. Pray for them today.

Group Meeting Following Week Six

The leader will plan the meeting to last no more than an hour and a half, arrange chairs in a circle, and welcome participants. Start on time.

FIRST:
- Invite participants to review their workbooks and select one or more of the following points to talk about:
- The day of the week that was most meaningful
- Your most significant learning of the week
- A question for the group to discuss now
- A "leading" you have to offer to the group

NEXT: As the workbook has guided us, you may have found yourself standing at home plate ready to bat. Do any (or all) of us want to make serious efforts to introduce spiritual discernment by consensus to our groups?

Notice the word *introduce*. This suggests making a beginning—even a simple beginning. The beginning may be a one-time presentation explaining discernment, or the idea may strike a chord with the group and involve lengthy commitment on your part. We have to start somewhere if we are to become a church that is trying to discern God's will for God's people.

How many in this group are ready to work with the four action steps listed in Day 3 of Week 6, page 111?

Allow 15–20 minutes for discussion on how to begin with these action steps: (1) Who will speak to which group? (2) When they will do it? (3) How much time will be required to set up the presentation and to speak? (4) What immediate goal does each person have in mind?

Let's take time to discuss how the silence has been going for you. Are you more—or less—comfortable with silence than before? Would you benefit from more silence in our worship services? What part do you feel silence should play in meetings at our church?

Closing Prayer Time

Have a sharing time, pray, and close with The Lord's Prayer.

The Local Congregation and the Higher Way

1. One of the biggest questions facing a congregation today is this: Is there a higher method of decision making than *Robert's Rules of Order*, which utilizes adversarial principles in an effort to seek unity? Can a local church improve itself by using a higher method? Can a church operate by spiritual discernment by consensus?

2. *There is no more pressing question facing a congregation than this:* If a congregation's prime concerns are institutional maintenance, ecclesiastical machinery, and "business as usual," then using the Standard Operating Procedure to ensure expediency and efficiency in decision making is OK. But what if the congregation is committed to finding a higher way to be the church?

3. What if the congregation's chief concerns—and needs—are vision, an ultimate purpose, and a sense of the divine will for a particular people in their corporate ministry and witness? How does a church manage such lofty matters? Is it proper to vote on a vision? Should a church choose up sides on an ultimate purpose? Do Christians overpower each other in a pursuit of the divine will? Sacred things must not be handled with soiled hands and clumsy methods.

4. The higher way for a church will seldom come through a vote. It will come about when it is spiritually discerned. But if we are stuck with a process based on a certain number of votes, we will be stuck with the outcome of the voting. I am not suggesting that *Robert's Rules of Order* is a bad or inferior method. It is an effective method of handling conflicting points of view. Many find it useful. But in some situations in the church *Rules* is not appropriate. We force certain questions and issues into the framework of *Robert's Rules of Order* that do not properly belong there. But we have no other choice as long as we have no other framework for considering a matter. I'm suggesting that *Robert's Rules* be skillfully used when it is needed without insisting that it is the only guide to decision making.

5. There *is* a higher way. *Spiritual discernment by consensus is possible for a congregation—of any size.*

6. Is a congregation fed up with carrying within its body the marks of the counterfeit church? Is there a church that has known a time when the powerful movement of the Holy Spirit made it unique and alive? On the other hand, is there a church that has never known spiritual vitality? Either of these could be the church that is willing to give itself to a new and higher way of being and doing. But how is it possible?

7. If the pastor and only a few others sense that discernment is a missing but needed factor, the beginning is possible. For now, the beginning is all that is necessary. Begin with one or two persons who will take seriously the quiet ministry of intercession for the congregation. The pastor will invite the congregation to share this vision and to begin preparations for becoming a church unique for its spiritual discernment. A vital pastoral function is to locate and enlist persons of prayer to give top priority in their prayer life to the knowing of God's will by God's people. United prayer for the vision of God for the people of God is a winning combination in any congregation. A church in Miami was blessed when a laywoman and the pastor met weekly to pray for the nominating committee and the Sunday school teachers.

8. Step by step, the progressive way toward spiritual discernment will be discerned by a loving prayer-force of faithful people. The following considerations would be important to a congregation seeking the higher way of spiritual discernment:

- Since this is a shift in fundamental orientation for the congregation, it will require time and faithful people of prayer—time to enlist people for prayer, time for people to pray for a new orientation.
- Change will be the order of the day because everything in the congregation's life will have to be evaluated and dealt with according to whether it makes the congregation authentically Christian or counterfeit. Considerations such as these are grist for the mill of spiritual discernment.
- This evaluation will be positive when every constituent group in the church evaluates itself to determine the level of spirituality at its heart. Each group will want to be candid about its own evaluation. The group that does not have healthy and recognizable spiritual vitality at its heart is a counterfeit Christian group and should either change or disband. The church is kidding itself when it is compromised

by elements within that betray its calling to be the body of Christ.

• It is important for a congregation to know whether an emphasis promotes or stifles Christian life! When the spiritual discernment is completed, what is not or cannot be done in a spirit of love should be discontinued. The only acceptable way to deal with such a question is through spiritual discernment.

9. The constituent group or organization that is positively responding to these criteria for spiritual authenticity will be preparing to become a spiritual discernment group—a little cell of aliveness within the church. Probably it will not be long before this group begins to discern what needs to be *spiritually discerned* compared to what needs to be decided. That is when and where the breakthrough begins.

10. Let's look in on a "business as usual" church board and watch how it handles an issue of vital concern for the congregation. The chair of the Work Area on Mission makes a recommendation from that group that the church sponsor a missionary through a mission special of $1000 a year. It may be a good idea whose time has come, since the church supports no missionary. But the motion is now at the mercy of an adversarial system. While most persons are thinking through the new idea, someone quickly speaks to oppose it; *the system is working.* Have you noticed how often the first person who speaks on a motion carries the vote? One lunge of opposition hits the proposal's jugular vein, followed by another negative voice, and the momentum is irreversible. In less than three minutes two people out of thirty-five have undone the work of the eight persons in the Work Area.

11. Count the losses: (1) A new idea never had a hearing; (2) the Work Area on Mission is repudiated and frustrated; (3) the members of the church board had no chance to think the idea through; (4) the congregation has no opportunity to show its interest in supporting a missionary; (5) the church has no personalized mission giving; and (6) the system that allowed this to happen is still in place.

12. Now let's look at how the church board would consider this from a perspective of spiritual discernment. The burden of decision is not on the church board only. Everyone is responsible for his or her own spiritual discernment.

13. First, the chair of the Work Area on Mission receives a notice about the need for specific missionary support (Step One). The spirituality of the Work Area on Mission is a microcosm of the whole church. They do not act only *on* a particular item of business, they act *for* the congregation in an effort to reflect, or call forth, the spiritual vitality of the church. Their evaluation of the proposed project turns on two points.

One: Will this project reflect and promote spiritual vitality at the heart of the church?

Two: Will this project be a valid way for our congregation to express our love for God and for persons in need (Step Two)?

14. At other times, proposals have been evaluated and dropped, but this idea rings true and is affirmed as a matter requiring prayer. Since the Work Area is composed of persons of prayer, their intercessions are focused upon the selected missionary and the congregation. Is this the will of God for our church? Yes or no? If confirmation comes, they decide to recommend the idea to the church board (Step Three).

15. The presentation includes facts, persons involved, type of ministry being supported, dollars, timing, and other details. But overshadowing all of these are the same ultimate questions: Is this a genuine expression of vital ministry for our congregation? Is there a better way to promote God's kingdom and express the spiritual vitality of our congregation? More specifically, is this God's will for us at this time (Step Four)? These are spiritual discernment questions. They should consider and pray about the proposal (Step Five).

16. We have looked at how two types of churches get their work done. There is no comparison, only vivid contrast between them; as much difference as night and day. I would be willing to trust the judgment that results from the spiritual discernment process and be guided by spiritually oriented persons whose first commitment is to know and do God's will. I would drive a long way (passing up several other churches if necessary) to participate in a congregation that was committed to this higher way of being and doing.

17. Where is such a church? A more important question to ask may be: How can my church become like that? *That is the question to ask the nominating committee.* If the criteria for nominations for the leaders of the church are higher than "business as usual," if persons are not selected just so slots can be filled, if offices and titles are not perfunctory and therefore cannot be filled by perfunctory people, and if the nominating committee does its work on the basis of spiritual discernment, there is great hope for the congregation.

18. The selection of a nominating committee composed of persons of prayer who will earnestly seek God's will for the church is supremely important in the life of a church committed to spiritual discernment. In fact, the selection of no other group is more important, for if the nominating committee does not give attention to the proper selection of leaders of the church, all other efforts to practice spiritual discernment will be counteracted. Spiritually oriented persons of prayer must be put into positions where they can properly consider questions requiring spiritual discernment or those positions must be left vacant!

19. I was pastor of a congregation that strove to become an authentic church. But selection of leadership was a key factor we had not addressed. Too many people in leadership roles were halfhearted and unexcited about the church and about their faith. With the bold conviction that we had to start at that point, I set this guideline for nominations: "We will not fill any position in the church that cannot be filled by persons in the spirit of love. If you are asked to take a responsibility, consider it carefully. Say no if you would accept it out of a sense of guilt, under pressure, or for ego reasons. Say no if you cannot do it in the spirit of love. We do not need anything done in the church that cannot be done in the spirit of love. We will leave unfilled any position that cannot be filled in the spirit of love!" The several unfilled positions were not missed. In fact their absence made the church stronger. If you and others decide that your church is a good place for spiritual discernment to become a concern, then a priority, and finally a way of life, it is possible for your congregation to function by the principles of spiritual discernment, regardless of its size.

Introduction to Exercises for Weeks Seven and Eight
Your Church Is Invited to Come Up to the Higher Way

Welcome to Week Seven and Week Eight of your workbook of spiritual discernment.

During Weeks Five and Six we crossed the bridge from personal to corporate discernment. A bridge is an apt metaphor for this movement because it links personal and corporate discernment by touching both simultaneously. The first five chapters were about personal discernment, which is essential if corporate discernment is to occur. The final three chapters are about corporate discernment that may be desired—even necessary—when more than one person is involved in making a decision.

We have now clearly crossed the bridge into corporate discernment. Bring all your experience with what you have learned about personal discernment with you as you look boldly at your congregation. See your church as a primary setting for inaugurating the practice of spiritual discernment.

You may be wondering what you—as only one person—can do. If you are a lay person, I can imagine your thinking: "Our pastor is the prime mover in something like this." And you are right!

If you are a pastor, you may be thinking, "If only a few lay persons in our church felt this way, we could begin immediately." And you also are right. We need each other—clergy and laity—to begin to shape the church of the future.

For now, begin with yourself. As you move through these two weeks in your workbook, think about what even you can do, and be thinking about others who might join you in the desire to move toward the higher way to be the church. Then perhaps you will be ready for the type of retreat described in Section Three, which outlines a format for a serious beginning experience in corporate discernment for your church.

Your Church Is Invited to Come Up to the Higher Way

Day 1: How to Begin the Higher Way

READING

Read Narrative Seven, *The Local Congregation and the Higher Way*.

Read paragraphs 7–9, pages 117–18.

Read Colossians 3:1–17.

REFLECTION AND RESPONSE

This passage from Colossians is a magnificent vision of how we are to be the church and what we are to do in the church. Select any specific changes you see your church will have to make if it is to become a church of spiritual discernment. List them here:

Begin with yourself. Are you ready to participate in the ministry of intercession for your church, and to call others into this ministry?

Pastor, numbers one and two on the list you just read are primarily for you. *Time* can be your enemy, or it can be your friend if you use it properly. And *change* can be a threat or a blessing, according to how you view it.

Lay Person, numbers three and four on the list are primarily for you. You are likely a member of one or more groups within your church. Is spiritual vitality found in all of them, any of them? What would happen if participants in one or all of your groups took this question seriously: *What is being done in this group in the spirit of love, and what is not?*

Now look carefully at your two secondary points on the list of four. Whether you are lay or clergy, all four are important for you to pray about: In prayer, with your pen in hand, consider any or all of the four points. Ask the Lord what you can do, specifically, to move

122

toward the higher way of spiritual discernment. As you pray and listen, write your thoughts here:

Day 2: Two Types of Churches

READING

Read paragraphs 10–16, pages 118–19.
Next, read Matthew 7:24–27.

REFLECTION AND RESPONSE

This may be the shortest daily exercise in your workbook—or it may become the longest.

First, focus on the image of the two houses from Matthew 7.

Next, look through the window of the business-as-usual church and the window of the church based on spiritual-discernment. Which would you rather be part of? Write your thoughts here: _____

_____

_____

Day 3: Digging Down to the Roots of Change

READING

Read paragraphs 17–19, pages 119–20.

REFLECTION AND RESPONSE

The important question is, "How can my church become like that?" Is that an important question for you? Really important? We are talking here about the possibility of systemic change in your church. Such change does not come easily or quickly.

If this is really important to you, two steps are essential: (1) Seek corporate strength, and (2) move into action. We will examine the first step today and the second tomorrow.

STEP ONE: SEEK CORPORATE STRENGTH

You need to discover whether anyone else shares your desire for your church to become a spiritual-discernment church. It is time to rally a prayer-force of intercessors who can begin prayerfully to discern the movement of the Spirit for the life of the congregation.

List below three intercessors you know you can depend on to prayerfully discern the movement of the Spirit in your congregation:

_____

_____

_____

Put a checkmark by one or more names of people you could comfortably ask, and will ask, to pray for spiritual discernment in the church.

What about your Discernment Workbook group? What do you think your group might do, corporately, to enhance the prayer life of your church? Write your thoughts here:

Step one is vital. See to it!

Day 4: Move Into Action

READING

Read again paragraphs 17–18, pages 119–20.

REFLECTION AND RESPONSE

Today and tomorrow we will examine two attitudes that may be barriers to overcome. Both are potent because they are often held by well-meaning people.

Barrier No. 1: There is a *natural resistance to change*, so you must be gentle about offering the "new approach to holding meetings." *Consider these observations*:

• The place of prayer in corporate spiritual discernment is so essential that without it there is no chance of succeeding.

• Varieties of prayer experiences touch people in different ways. Variety may be expressly called for because the issues that need to be considered will also vary.

• The value an ongoing group within the church places on silence in community is an indicator of spiritual maturity.

• Silence that focuses on prayer prepares the group to be together at a deeper level of presence to each other and to God.

With these observations before you, what additional insights do you have about the place of prayer—or lack of it—in your selected group within the church? Write your comments here:

Review the observations you have just written and compare

them with the ones listed above in this exercise. Are they calling you to do anything? What is it?

_____

_____

_____

STEP TWO: MOVE INTO ACTION

Just thinking will not make it so. Action is needed. Has someone talked with the pastor about corporate spiritual discernment? With the lay leader? With the chair of the church board?

Who is the chair of the nominations committee? Who is on the committee? All of them need to be contacted. They need to be talked with lovingly about the importance of selection of members of the nominating committee and those whom they nominate.

Prayerful support and patience is needed as you share this new vision of the importance of nominating spiritually oriented persons for leadership in the church. The risk that nominating committee members will misunderstand your intentions and possibly feel threatened require that this effort be saturated in prayer.

To think that we must have a church structured on spiritual-discernment even at the expense of casualities along the way is a total repudiation of spiritual discernment! It takes much prayer, lots of love, and time. We have a generous Source of all three, so begin today.

Close with a period of several minutes of silence to listen for a word from the Lord about what you should do.

Day 5: Facing the Old Order

READING

Begin to read Narrative Eight through "Correction To Barrier No. 1," pages 129–30.

Day 6: How Do You Feel About Consensus?

READING

Read "Barrier 2" and "Correction for Barrier 2," pages 130–32.

REFLECTION AND RESPONSE

Barrier No. 2 (the belief that consensus is impractical) is a major obstacle because this attitude may be held by a majority of your people. Even you may feel that consensus is impractical.

If that is true for you, you may wish to look again at the content under "Corrections To Barrier No. 2." Consensus is a radical approach to decision making and will require a radical change in attitude and procedure for you and many others. Try to incorporate the idea of consensus by spiritual discernment not only in your surface understanding, but also in your deeper consciousness.

Do not try to *convince* another person that this is a better way. It is more effective to *share* the concept of spiritual discernment by consensus! The concept has power of its own, and if you interpret it well, the concept will draw others to itself.

Review the reading for today mentioned above and decide how you feel about consensus. Write your thoughts here:

If you are having difficulty defining consensus, you may wish to ask another member of the group to discuss the concept. Do so now. Then summarize your conversation and thoughts here:

As you prepare for tomorrow's workbook session, schedule adequate time to complete the exercise before you go to church. Be seated in the sanctuary a few minutes early so you will have some time for silence to focus on worship.

Day 7: Your Part/Their Part

READING

Read again 1 Corinthians 12:12–31.

REFLECTION AND RESPONSE

This is the same Scripture you read last Sunday.

Paul's strong illustration of "body parts" beginning in verse 12 is underscored in verses 27 through 31. Whatever else this passage says to us, one message is clear: Each of us is an important part of the body of Christ; therefore, we are responsible for faithfulness in *being* the important part we are. You do not have to do it all—just your part.

Everyone who worships with you today is also a part of the body of Christ. Many do not understand this, but they may know in their hearts that there must be more to their faith than they have experienced.

You can help them as you worship today. When you have settled into your place of worship, take a few minutes to watch people as they come into church. Pick out four or five persons and pray silently for them by name, that they will increasingly know the part they are in the body of Christ and be faithful.

Group Meeting Following Week Seven

The leader will plan the meeting to last no more than an hour and a half, arrange chairs in a circle, and welcome participants. Start on time.

FIRST: Invite participants to review their workbooks and select one or more of the following points to talk about:
- The day of the week that was most meaningful.
- Something significant learned this week.
- A question for the group to discuss.
- Any loose ends from previous sessions.

NEXT: Ask participants to relax and reflect upon these past weeks. What has happened to your church? What has happened to this group? What has happened to you? Since we are all one family, talk candidly about the strengths and weaknesses of this group for each person and for the group as a whole. (Allow about ten minutes for sharing.)

FINALLY:
- What specific changes for your church did you list on Day 1 of Week Seven?
- What concern facing this church can best be handled through the five steps listed in the reading for Day 2?
- What can this group do to be helpful—and not misunderstood—in encouraging the nominating committee to function as suggested on Day 3?

Spend five minutes in silence by holding in your mind the image of your church becoming a church of spiritual discernment. After the silence, share prayerful insights that came to you in the silence. Close with The Lord's Prayer.

Shaping the Church of the Future

The church is changing! Not all churches, I am sorry to say, but some are. Far too many remain committed to the secular slogan "business as usual." This usually brings two results: First, the church is run like a business but with the unhappy result that there is more loss than gain. Second, everything about that church is very "usual," with little sense of fulfillment or excitement.

But many churches are changing because they have begun to put special emphasis upon corporate and personal spirituality. By doing this they discover a bright and promising future and a fulfilling present marked by a spiritual dynamism known for its creativity, excitement, and power. Becoming a church based on spiritual discernment is one of the keys to keeping your church from being run like a business, which at its heart it is not.

To become a church based on spiritual discernment, begin with little steps and let time work for you. There is no need to push. Rejoice that your church does not have to remain as it has always been. You can begin now to shape a new and exciting future by realizing that new depths of spiritual reality have been promised to you. If you want to discover and claim this deeper reality, begin to shape your church into the church of the future. Resistance will come because existing patterns and relationships are not easily changed. So count on it and discover ways to deal with it.

Let me describe six real and potent barriers to becoming a spiritually discerning church. Each barrier or problem is followed by a sentence or two to illustrate how the barrier might be verbalized. Then an approach to deal with the barrier is suggested.

BARRIER NO. 1: PEOPLE RESIST CHANGE.

Why isn't the way we have decided things all these years OK? That is the way we have gotten where we are.

CORRECTION TO BARRIER NO. 1: LEARN A NEW
APPROACH TO CONDUCTING MEETINGS.

The new approach is steeped in prayer. That is its distinguishing
characteristic. Daily devotional practices of members of boards,
committees, choirs, prayer groups, and Sunday school classes will be
affected. Another dimension is the presence and style of prayer that
characterizes the group when it gathers. Instead of the ceremonial
prayer to open the meeting, there could be prayerful reading
(praying) of some Psalms as a primary focus of the meeting. The
group's leader can gently increase the length of time for silence and
prayer, to prepare the group to "be together" and to "listen." These
varied prayer experiences should not be treated as "preliminaries"
but as essentials that set the tone of the meeting. If, eventually, the
first fifteen to twenty minutes of every meeting is spent in worship
and prayer and silence to focus the group on discernment, the time
that follows will be highly productive.

BARRIER NO. 2: CONSENSUS IS IMPRACTICAL.

*You can seldom get people to agree, and if they did, would we be
better off with "yes people"? Wouldn't they be reluctant to say how
they really feel about an issue when such a premium is put on
consensus? A person who opposes something that everyone else
agrees on could feel bad.*

CORRECTION TO BARRIER NO. 2: CLEARLY
UNDERSTAND THE CONSENSUS PRINCIPLE.

Consensus is one of the principles used by the Quakers
(Friends) who have specialized in spiritual discernment for over
three hundred years and have much to teach us.

Consensus means general agreement on a particular matter. At
times in church meetings we reach unanimity by common consent or,
more formally, by vote. But what about those times when the house
is divided? Our standard procedure is to negotiate and bargain and
amend and substitute, until a trend has been established and a vote
taken. The issue can be decided on the strength of one vote over fifty
percent. We experienced this bare majority in the worst way when
we started a new church and decided to vote on two popular names
for it. In the final vote, a majority of two made the decision. That
meant that half the congregation, minus three, didn't like the name
that was selected. Why couldn't the decision have been delayed in an
effort to find the name that would have been right for more, most, or
all of the people?

The Friends do it differently. They wait for the inner prompting of the Spirit and share their "leading." If not everyone confirms the leading, their reasons are considered, allowing for the possibility of reshaping the leading. Consensus among Friends does not mean that such a process continues until absolutely everyone can and does agree. Sometimes it means that a leading is reshaped until a consensus *not to block it* prevails. A Friend may say, "I am not totally satisfied so that I can enthusiastically support the proposition, but I feel good enough so that I am not compelled to oppose it in order to be true to my conscience."

Or a proposition may do violence at a deeper level of conscience. A Friend may request that his or her name be registered in opposition to the proposition. That does not derail the matter, but it puts the community on notice of a deep concern.

The provision for Friends to dissent by allowing their names to be registered in opposition is an expression of inclusion. When the dissent is *included*, the relationship is intact and can still influence the community and the individual. Compare that to the broken relationships that frequently occur on matters of deep concern when there are winners and losers after our votes are counted.

With Friends, influence may also move from the individual to the group. For example, from 1745 onward, John Woolman, as a matter of conscience, spoke out against slavery. He called upon the Friends who were present to free their slaves. There was no consensus, but he was not the only one who felt that leading. Others took the opposite position and could not accept his leading. He went on record in opposition to Friends holding slaves, but the Friends Meeting (their church) counted him in and honored his leading. They said in effect, "We cannot accept it for ourselves, but we want you to follow your leading. We will do your work, tend your crops, look after your family, and provide you with income to free you to travel the land and call Friends to free their slaves." They did just that for twenty years while John Woolman went up and down the Atlantic coast doing what God had called him to do. And Quakers freed their slaves more than a century before the Civil War.

Spiritual discernment by consensus will probably not be an easier or quicker way for the group to do its work. Also, many groups in the church with potential for spiritual discernment do not have business items and long-range decisions to make, e.g., a prayer group. But whether the group has "work" to do or not, every group in the church is called to utilize spiritual discernment as its way for people to be together; to care for the goals, interests, and concerns of its participants; and to be a vital spiritual factor within the congregation.

BARRIER NO. 3: THE CHURCH IS LIKE A BUSINESS.

Worship, prayer, choir, and tithing are all one type of thing, but the business affairs of the church are different. But tough decisions about money require tough-minded people.

CORRECTION TO BARRIER NO. 3: TRAIN LEFT-BRAIN PEOPLE TO DO RIGHT-BRAIN WORK.

Many in responsible decision-making positions in the church are predominantly left-brained in their orientation—they approach decisions on an analytical, cognitive, problem-solving, scientific-method basis. They are accustomed to adding things up—one, two, three—and that is that! "Just lay out the facts and let's get on with it." This is good because spiritual discernment thrives on a left-brain orientation—when it is enhanced with the thinking of right-brain persons. In the church, each needs the other.

Not all church business is left-brain work. Some is. Right-brain people have the souls of poets. They long for reflective time to be able to see beneath the surface of the facts, and usually spiritual-discernment issues are right-brain issues. The problem in the church is that we ask left-brain people to decide right-brain issues, while not allowing time or settings for right-brain people to function at *the point of their strength*. The church needs to structure learning opportunities to help left-brain people cultivate their right-brain potential instead of the other way around. Left-brain decisions will get made—the left-brain people will see to that. But right-brain discernments will be lacking unless the church sees to it that all are encouraged to become discerners of the Spirit.

BARRIER NO. 4: THE PASTOR IS IN CHARGE.

The People

We expect strong leadership from our pastor, the spiritual leader of our congregation. Our pastor determines the direction for our church to move. If we didn't feel that the pastor is doing a good job we would ask for a change because we know that the church is really an extension of the pastor.

The Pastor

My people expect me to be a leader in the church and the community. I feel the weight of this responsibility. I can make good decisions and plans for the future of the congregation when I am not overrushed and overtired.

CORRECTION TO BARRIER NO. 4: THE "PASTOR IN CHARGE" FINDS A HIGHER WAY TO BE THE PASTOR.

As a clergyman for thirty-five years and pastor for twenty-two, I know the significance of the term "pastor in charge": the denomination holds the pastor responsible for the church's well-being. It also refers to the way the pastor relates to the congregation. At best, this concept is translated into a firm hand running a tight ship, being a strong leader. At worst, it can mean control in negative ways such as domination and manipulation.

But being the pastor in charge can also be taken personally. It can mean to be in charge of oneself; that is, to have a sense of personal maturity and centeredness that affirms confidence in people as they mature in the practice and process of discernment. To be in charge is also to be free in one's relationship with God, to recognize that God is ultimately in charge, and consistently to model that awareness in one's life and ministry.

The people and the pastor take a risk when they depend upon the Holy Spirit. There is uncertainty in a new kind of vulnerability between pastor and people and between people and people. Flack may be generated, and strong feelings that the old way was more familiar, less risky, and therefore better, may surface.

We are talking about a higher way to be the pastor. This may mean a radical shift of consciousness or involve the pastor and the people in a dramatic shift in their understanding of God. The shifts must be tempered with prayer, gentleness, caution, and time. And any change must be guided by a powerful vision—the vision of pastoring a church where it is normal for the Holy Spirit to reveal the will of God to the people of God. Compare that vision to what your congregation is like now. Ask yourself whether there is enough difference and promise to make you want to be such a pastor (or to have such a pastor) and pursue the vision.

BARRIER NO. 5: NATURAL LEADERS AND POWER PEOPLE IN THE CHURCH CONTROL DECISIONS.

Natural leaders have learned by experience that if you have a plan most people will fall into line with it. They see no need to wait for consensus.

CORRECTION TO BARRIER NO. 5: LAY LEADERSHIP
FINDS A HIGHER WAY TO BE THE CHURCH.

The "right" person's opinion makes a big difference in how an
issue is perceived and, usually, its outcome. This is good! After all,
we look for leadership and we can honor natural leaders who put
their weight behind a project. We look to them also for wisdom,
fairness, and farsightedness.

Power can become an obsession for some, however. They have
learned that people and situations can be exploited and manipulated.
Both natural leaders and power people are usually fully functional in
the life of the congregation. The spiritual-discernment mode of being
and doing can be frustrating to both types.

Consider the natural leader: In the church committed to
spiritual discernment, more people will invariably be "elevated" into
leadership, and that calls for creation of room at the top. More
people will be involved in decisions as they embrace spiritual
discernment, a radical change when followers become spiritual
leaders.

For the power person, the shift may also be threatening. In the
church committed to spiritual discernment, there is little opportunity
for manipulating the adversarial method by choosing up sides or
using clever parliamentary maneuvers. When people are called to
pray, to wait upon each other in love, to listen to the Holy Spirit, and
to long to know the will of God on a given issue, everything is
different. No more cronyism, no lining up the votes, no arm-twisting
persuasion.

Spiritual discernment by consensus is an entirely new way of
being and doing for power people, natural leaders, and almost
everyone else. The potential outcome of the discernment model is
like a gift to make the heart glad. Let me illustrate as I describe a
final barrier that must be overcome if you are to have a church
committed to spiritual discernment.

BARRIER NO. 6: BUSY PEOPLE FAVOR BRIEF
MEETINGS.

*Spiritual discernment takes lots of time. Our people are busy with
many responsibilities and are accustomed to making decisions and
moving forward. That is the kind of person we need when we are
deciding the future of the church. If we are not careful, we could
drive away our strongest leaders by dragging out our meetings.*

CORRECTION TO BARRIER NO. 6: CHURCH LEADERSHIP MUST DECIDE WHETHER IT PRIZES EXPEDIENCY OR SPIRITUAL GUIDANCE.

As I have mentioned, spiritual discernment by consensus is not a quicker way, but it is a better way. Here is an actual case in point.

The Leadership Team for the second Nashville Academy had a difference of opinion about the crowded daily schedule. We had lived with the same struggle during the two years of the first Nashville Academy, and we found no way to relieve the crowded agenda without giving up something more important than freedom from fatigue. Some on the new Leadership Team felt it was time to bite the bullet, give up a prized feature, and get on with the change. Others could not agree and we were stalemated. It looked as if we would be polarized because competing positions were strongly supported. If we had voted, we would have had winners and losers on the team and among participants in the Academy.

The thing that saved us was the discernment mode to which we were committed. At our final meeting we agreed—we covenanted—with each other to make this issue a matter of earnest prayer during the three months before we met again. When the team reassembled, we began with a period of silence to center ourselves in the Holy Spirit and be present with each other. We called for reports of leadings of the Spirit. What followed was almost unbelievable. *No one advocated previously held positions!* We discovered that no one had talked to another member about the issue. We had prayed about it and we had listened, and in less than twelve minutes the matter was resolved. The solution had eluded the Advisory Board for a year and a half, the previous Leadership Team for two and a half years, and me for almost a year. We found a way to cut an hour off the schedule.

Besides discerning a great solution, we learned something wonderful: *Spiritual discernment is a higher and better way.* Expediency and efficiency in decision making had given way to a deep commitment to spiritual guidance. Disagreement was frustrating but nothing like the anxiety and problems that would have followed any number of poor solutions.

Your Church Is Invited to Come Up to the Higher Way, Part Two

Day 1: Dealing With Strong Opinions

READING

Read "Barrier No. 3" through "Correction to Barrier No. 3," page 132.

REFLECTION AND RESPONSE

Have you ever heard someone say, "The church is like a business"? A church does not have to be large before it adopts business practices and terminology: organization, accounting procedures, efficiency, audits, written reports, etc. There are two reasons for this: (1) Business practices and terminology are essential in a church; and (2) left-brain people who use them are abundant and usually outspoken in leadership.

Look at adjectives that describe left-brain people: analytical, cognitive, problem-solving. Their motto seems to be "Just lay out the facts and let's make a decision and get on with it."

Now consider adjectives that describe right-brain people: affective, poetic, reflective.

Are you left brain or right brain? _____

Think of the group within the church that you selected on Day 6 of Week 5. Are most of the people in it right-brain or left-brain persons? _____

Think about this as you make your plans.

Day 2: The Pastor in Charge

READING

Read "Barrier No. 4" and "Correction to Barrier No. 4," pages 132–33.

REFLECTION AND RESPONSE

About the pastor of the church virtually everyone has a strong opinion—including the pastor! The pastor's role, methods, leadership skills, relational abilities and overall effectiveness are properly and finally determined by *vision*: The pastor's vision of ministry and the people's vision of ministry

The in-charge factor is critical because everyone is affected by it. It means control. Being in control of people, events, programs, and decisions does not necessarily mean one is exercising effective pastoral leadership.

In a church committed to spiritual discernment, the ultimate need is the vision to recognize that God is in charge and consistently to model that awareness in one's life and ministry. This vision should be shared by pastor and people. Strongly held opinions may be positive or negative, whereas vision is likely to be positive.

Here is where you can help to overcome barriers. Close today with a time of prayer that a new vision be given to your people, a vision of what it means to be a spiritually sensitive and spiritually alive congregation. After your time of prayer, use the space here to write any ideas that came to you:

Day 3: Working With People

READING

Read "Barrier No. 5" and "Corrections to Barrier No. 5," pages 133–34.

REFLECTION AND RESPONSE

Let's face it, people are the church, and their attitudes and motives are either helps or hindrances. The shift from the adversarial to the spiritual-discernment approach may bring a major upheaval in patterns of relationship, the politics of action—or inaction—and a personal sense of identity for many people. Naïveté is unaffordable at this point. You need to know that when rules of relationship are changed, everyone becomes uncomfortable. Are you ready for upheaval? No one can say how pronounced it will be or how long it will take for things to settle down. Therefore, you need to take the long look in this matter of potential upheaval. Move with care, for there is no quick remedy for hurt feelings or a sense of being threatened.

What can you do to help? List here all the jobs, responsibilities, or functions you have in the church.

_____

_____

_____

How do you feel about giving these up if it becomes necessary? Be realistic in your assessment, and put a check mark by all that you could freely and lovingly give up in order to make room at the top. Do not check any that you could not easily give up.

IF there are any unchecked jobs, responsibilities, or functions, take time now for prayer to help sort out your feelings. *IF* you checked all of your jobs, try to think of others who might feel threatened by changes in their roles. Name one of those in your time of prayer. Pray that he or she will enhance change rather than being a barrier to change.

Day 4: Prayer Is the Key

READING

Read "Barrier No. 6" and "Corrections to Barrier No. 6," pages 134–35.

REFLECTION AND RESPONSE

Prayer has been the dominant theme throughout this week. The illustration in today's reading turned at the point of *prayer for spiritual guidance.* Prayer is the key!

What was the last issue that persons in your selected group took as a corporate prayer concern?

_____

When? _____

Are you willing to present a prayer concern to your selected group? If so, think of something specific and significant for the entire group. This can be an extension of the effort you planned last week to introduce spiritual discernment to your group. Write it here:

_____

_____

Now make specific plans for presenting the prayer concern to your group. Think of such details as date, time, your reason for sharing it, and how long you want your group to pray about it. Write your notes here: _____

_____
_____
_____

Close your time now with a prayer for additional guidance and follow through on steps to present your prayer concern.

Day 5: Evaluation

READING
Take a few minutes to read the major themes of the previous seven weeks in your workbook. This is a way to review the flow of content in the workbook and the flow of your response and involvement in spiritual discernment.

REFLECTION AND RESPONSE
Write responses to these questions in spaces provided:
(1) Evaluate your participation in this group. Summarize your fervor or lack of it, level of regularity in following the workbook; the manner in which you let it scratch beneath the surface of your experience.

(2) How will this study influence the way you make decisions?

(3) What difference will it make in your selected group?

(4) What difference in your church?

(5) What is your church's alternative to the discernment mode?

Day 6: Do You Have an Urge to Go On?

READING
Read 1 Corinthians 12:27–31.

REFLECTION AND RESPONSE

The question before all the participants in this group is a big *now what?* You have given major consideration to three significant concepts: personal spiritual discernment, corporate spiritual discernment, and a lower way and a higher way to be the church. You have also made plans (and perhaps taken initial steps) to introduce the higher way of spiritual discernment.

But there is more. Paul writes, " . . . eagerly desire the higher gifts." Do you want to join others in your group in a combined effort to invite the leaders of your church to consider seriously how to become a church characterized by spiritual discernment?

Discuss that possibility further at the next group session. You will want to be present for this significant meeting. *Before that be sure to read "Beginning To Shape the Church of the Future" beginning on page 148.* Reflect on the value of a retreat for your congregation and be prepared to begin during your next group meeting to discern steps you and your group are ready to take.

As you prepare for tomorrow's workbook exercise, schedule adequate time to complete it before you go to church today. Be seated in the sanctuary a few minutes early so you will have some quality silence to center in for worship.

Day 7: A Last (or Is it First?) Look at Your Church

> **Note:** It is important that you complete today's workbook exercise before you go to church.

READING

Read again 1 Corinthians 12:12–31.

REFLECTION AND RESPONSE

During the Sundays of our study together, we have come week after week to this same passage. Perhaps it has taken on more special meaning for you. Do you see anything in this passage that you did not see when you began reading it? Read back over the passage and note in the space below any word, verse, or idea that has new significance for you:

In light of this passage, do you see your congregation differently now than before? As today's title suggests, this could be the last look you have at your church in the light of this study—because the discipline of using the workbook ends today. But it could also be your first look if you are beginning to see it differently. Think and then write about your ideas, dreams, and hopes for a "new" church:

Group Meeting Following Week Eight

The leader will plan the meeting to last no more than an hour and a half, arrange chairs in a circle, and welcome participants. Start on time.

A Refreshing Note

Since this is the last meeting scheduled for this group, refreshments will be welcome for a fellowship time. They should be served when they won't interfere with the flow of the meeting.

Invite participants to share their feelings about their last four weeks together. End the sharing with five minutes of silence in which to give thanks for each other and your common journey. After the silence ask for comments about what silence has meant to them (not what it is *supposed* to have meant). During this period, call for comments from those who want to tell about their progress on plans and actions.

The big question before the group is *now what?* The leader will call for agreement on the next step.

Here are suggestions:

(1) End the group with this meeting. Everyone is on his or her own for personal follow-through.

(2) Continue the group until participants have taken steps to carry out the plans made on Day Three of this week and have presented the reports. Depending on the results of their actions, the group may choose at that time to continue to meet to help make and carry out additional plans.

(3) Decide now to join with others in your church who have studied or are studying this workbook, and make a united effort to follow through on the plan set forth in Section Three, *Beginning To Shape the Church of the Future.*

Each activity is of value, but it is obvious that the third option has the greatest potential for permanent impact upon the future of your church.

If Number 2 is the consensus choice, do the following at this meeting:

Determine how often and how long the workbook group will

continue to meet. Determine the type of meeting: prayer group, study group, spiritual-discernment strategy group, etc. The new group will flourish for four to six weeks with its beginning momentum. At that point it will be wise to review participants' progress and the group's purpose, and set a new timeline for the group.

If the group chooses Number 3, do the following at this meeting:

1. Make certain that everyone has read Section Three, *Beginning To Shape the Church of the Future.*

2. Summarize the main points of the proposal in Section Three.

3. If your pastor is not studying this workbook, plan to meet with the pastor to seek his or her wholehearted cooperation and support for the following four steps. But if the pastor opposes the following plan, the group is ill-advised to proceed until a spirit of cooperation has been carefully cultivated.

Plan for Shaping the Church of the Future

Step One: All participants (in all workbook groups) begin to introduce the concept of spiritual discernment by consensus in selected groups that were chosen in Week Six. Estimate when this step will begin and how long you anticipate it will take—perhaps no longer than a month to six weeks.

Step Two: Set regular meeting times for the discernment group(s) to meet—preferably weekly, no less than fortnightly.

Step Three: With the cooperation of the pastor, chair of the church board, nominating committee, and other key leaders, plan for an all-day church-wide leadership retreat four to six months from now. Include the church board, Council on Ministries, or similar body, all leaders of Sunday school classes, choirs, small groups, etc.

Step Four: Adapt the guidelines found in Section Three as the format for developing your "Beginning To Shape the Church of the Future" retreat.

These four steps are too much to accomplish in one meeting. Go as far as you can. Be sure that everyone has a good overview of the four major steps above. Set the next meeting date and review details of responsibilities assigned in preparation for that meeting. Put a priority on the responsibility you accept and upon attendance at the group meetings. Primary agenda items for the next several meetings are a systematic study of Section Three and a carefully developed strategy for adapting and implementing the plan described in Section Three.

Closing the Meeting

• *If you are a singing group*, sing something appropriate for the occasion.

• *If you are a fun-loving group*, think of possibilities for the future of your church and shout, "Hooray!"

• *If you are a hungry group* (and refreshments have been prepared), begin to practice the Vow of Fellowship—"A fondness for eating with special friends."

You may choose to do all three of the above!

After the refreshments have been served, end the time of conviviality with the Lord's Prayer.

A Retreat Format

Preface to Section Three

It is possible for a congregation of any size to operate on the basis of spiritual discernment!

If I did not believe this, I would not have written this book. However, you may not believe it at this point in our consideration of discernment. In fact, you may never believe that your church can operate like this. I will be encouraged if you and many others in your congregation become convinced.

Right now I will have achieved my purpose if there is even a slight hope among you that there is a better and higher way of decision making and charting the ministry of your church than the adversarial method. What if it is true that there actually is a higher and better way and that it is workable in your church? Are you dissatisfied and frustrated with the way decisions are currently made?

I would settle for even that much concern and intent. Even a simple gnawing agitation that there may be a better way can work like a grain of sand in an oyster—and bring forth a pearl in your church!

If you are not at that point now, in fairness to you, I must tell you that there is no reason for you to read further, for in Section Three is a plan for actually shaping the church of the future on the discernment model. If that is not where you are, drop out here and continue to work with the personal practices of discernment we studied during the first five weeks.

Beginning to Shape the Church of the Future

We have come a long way since we began our study of discernment. But compared to where we can go from this point, our previous progress will seem like a pre-game warm-up. Progress may be slow for a while but hold steady. The goal is great enough to merit the efforts you and others will put forth.

As you finished Week Eight you committed yourself to be an advocate for spiritual discernment within one (or maybe more) of your favorite groups. That is an important commitment because what we do now will stand on the shoulders of that beginning effort.

THE GOALS

- Combine the efforts and focus the energy of persons who want seriously to consider the proposition that spiritual discernment by consensus is a higher and better way for your church.

- Plan a retreat so that your leaders can begin to face the question, "Is this workable in our church?"

THE PROCESS

1. At the retreat, you will comb through this workbook and glean insights and principles that apply to your church.

2. We will look specifically at two classical models of discernment—the Ignatian model and the Quaker model, and carefully select insights that you will find useful.

THE PLAN

Several guidelines are suggested here for planning your retreat. They will present your leadership with an experiential introduction to viable spiritual-discernment principles in a flexible format. After the retreat, your leaders can select the steps they are ready to take.

Planning the Retreat

- Discuss with your pastor, lay leader, chairs of the church board, the committee on nominations, and other leaders the urgency of selecting the date and location for the retreat. A minimum of eight hours will be necessary; allow more time if possible. It may be more comfortable to have an hour and a half to two-hour session on Friday evening after a church supper and six or more hours on Saturday. Plan to serve a continental breakfast and a light lunch. Provide for a morning break if you schedule six hours on Saturday, a morning and afternoon break for a one-day retreat.

• A strong Retreat Planning Committee is needed to care for details of meals, registration, transportation (if needed), program of the retreat, and follow-up. The committee should include some who are members of the workbook group and some who are not.

Make the retreat a high visibility, priority event to rally interest and attendance.

• When the retreat is announced, the Retreat Planning Committee will begin immediately to make plans to follow up on efforts of participants in the workbook group(s) to introduce the concept of spiritual discernment. Between now and the retreat, many groups can begin to utilize simple principles of spiritual discernment by:

(1) Freely discussing the concepts in preparation for the retreat.

(2) Selecting practices to begin implementing, such as:

- Choosing a few concerns/interests for the group to pray about over a stated period of time.

- Introducing and observing periods of silence when the group gathers, and encouraging personal, daily periods of silence.

- Discussing the ultimate goal the group wants to accomplish within a given time frame. Setting the goal makes it possible for the group to begin to discern in earnest whether *the suggested goal is God's will for this group.*

Plans to follow up the efforts to introduce discernment and to prepare for the retreat are essential. Change will come slowly but participants will experience a new way to be the church.

Before the retreat, the following will be helpful:

- Creative and frequent announcements about the retreat

- Sermons by the pastor(s) that interpret spiritual discernment and challenge the church to consider "the higher way"

- Distribution of copies of this workbook with encouragement for all who will attend the retreat to read the narratives.

A FURTHER NOTE BEFORE BEGINNING

Prepare thoroughly before the retreat so that the retreat program will move unhurriedly but deliberately through program options.

Decide in advance about any components of the retreat program that you may have to omit. Plan to offer omitted components to various groups in the church after the retreat.

Long before the retreat the committee should carefully select leaders for the various components of the program so that they will be well prepared for leadership. Choose leaders for:

- Easy-to-sing choruses

- Singing, chanting, or praying the Psalms

- Reading and interpreting Genesis 28:10–22

- Reading "Clearly Understand the Consensus Principle" beginning on page 130

- Reviewing the Ignatian method of discernment and a discussion (see Narrative Two, pages 41ff.)

- Reviewing the Quaker Committee of Clearness (see Narrative Two)

- Summarizing "Two Types of Churches" in paragraphs 10–16, pages 118f.

Be sure the chair of the nominating committee is prepared to explain the role of the committee.
Select EXCELLENT leaders!

Holding the Retreat

The Retreat Coordinator should be sensitive to the pace of the schedule and to the participants' need and desire for fellowship and relaxation. Take brief breaks when you feel they are needed. With the assistance of a good music leader spend brief periods singing familiar choruses. Allow about forty-five minutes for lunch.

Strive for an unhurried and unstrained beginning for the program of the retreat itself. The entire retreat should be characterized by an easygoing style. The goal is to begin to model a way of being together that is not time-managed or results-driven. Time is important and so are results. But spiritual discernment is also important, and we need to learn to be together in ways that make it possible for all three to be honored.

For creative expression, make a point of inviting participants who use creative aids to sculpt symbolic expressions of the retreat or an inspirational or humorous piece. You may decide to provide modeling clay, assorted colors of pipe stem cleaners, and flexible, lightly coated, small-gauge wire cut in twelve- and eighteen-inch lengths. If these are provided, tables will be necessary. Otherwise, place chairs in a large circle. At the end of the retreat, take time to share the symbols and to discuss the value of this affective, right-brain form of expression.

- Begin the retreat with a warm welcome and easy-to-sing choruses (no more than ten minutes for both).

- State the purpose of the retreat as simply as possible. Allow five minutes for silence, asking the group to think and pray about the purpose.

- Ask how many persons have read the workbook narratives and how many have completed the entire workbook.

- Introduce the person selected to lead in singing or praying a selected Psalm. This person should be well prepared, since this may be the first time some have experienced this form of prayer.

Note: *The Upper Room Worshipbook* contains Psalm settings (with antiphons) appropriate for reading, chanting, or singing. You will need at least one copy for use in the retreat.

- Call on the person you asked to prepare to read and interpret Genesis 28:10–22. Highlight the significance for discernment of verses 16–17. (Only the angels in Jacob's dream used the ladder, but through discernment Jacob could "see" and "hear" that "the Lord is in this place." And he had not known it.)

> To recognize when "the Lord is in this place"—and when the Lord is not—is the goal of a church committed to spiritual discernment.

- In groups of four or five, consider these three questions with seven to ten minutes of discussion:

Question One: *When in the church have you been aware that "the Lord is in this place?" How?*

Question Two: *When have you known that the Lord was not in this place—or this discussion, etc.? How?*

Question Three: *How did the entire group know that?*

• Take about fifteen minutes to focus on vision as you read to the group two or three of the following Scripture passages, allowing time for silence after two or three selections. Ask participants to use the creative aids of clay, wire, etc., during the silence to begin to form an image or a symbol of their church. These creations should be based upon the Scripture passages. Choose from Acts 2:42–47; Luke 4:16–19; Matthew 25:31–40; Romans 12; Ephesians 4:1–16, and others you may select.

If your retreat begins on Friday night, this is a good place to stop for the evening. This first section of retreat content is about seventy-five minutes long. If you are in a retreat setting, the group's energy will have been devoted to travel, moving in, settling down, and making a good beginning the first evening. Don't overtire the group by presenting too much content at this point or by otherwise exerting pressure.

TRYING OUT SPIRITUAL DISCERNMENT BY CONSENSUS FOR A GOOD PURPOSE

• Spend ample time during the retreat to select major discernment issues in the current life of the congregation. It may not be possible to accomplish this within the time allowed. Simply to begin to try to discern will be a major accomplishment.

How the group tries to discern is also important. *Make it clear that we want to discern this congregation's greatest needs or concerns. Remind the group that we wish to be open to the Holy Spirit and to each other so that we can know and agree on what is most important in our church.*

• To begin this process, divide into groups of five (groups of three if fewer than twenty-five persons are present). Ask each group to join hands while seated in a circle. Call for silence and prayer (ten minutes) and ask participants to be open to what the Spirit has to say about the most basic needs of the church.

• After the silence, allow groups about five minutes to select *one great concern of the congregation* that they feel needs discernment. Write all choices on the chalkboard.

The object is to have several major choices for the entire group to consider so that it can select the three most important interests or concerns. Write them on the chalk board.

• Ask someone to read "Clearly Understand the Consensus Principle" on pages 130ff.

• Allow about an hour for prayer and openness to the Holy Spirit and to each other as you apply the consensus principle to selection of one concern or issue for discernment. If consensus cannot be reached in the allotted time, do not despair. You have been together in a wonderful way (a higher way) and this effort can be continued in the weeks ahead.

• As important as identifying at the final major interest or concern in the life of the church is, you want to focus on the **process of discernment** in which the group just participated. Take a few minutes to review what you have just done and how you did it. What are the implications for your ongoing life together?

DECISION AND DISCERNMENT, PART ONE

The previous exercise has been, or will be, productive in helping you to agree about some major direction or emphasis for your congregation. It may change eventually, but for now this is a worthy selection.

Your selection may be an affirmation of God's will. Possibly, for example, "It is God's will that our church remain where it is instead of building in a new location." Or your selection may call you to discern God's will: "Is it God's will that we stay in this location or move to another?"

Let this discernment issue serve as a case in point as you consider how to use the Ignatian method of discernment described in paragraphs 7ff. on pages 42ff.

- Ask the person who is prepared to review the Ignatian method to lead a discussion on how it can aid you in discernment. Carefully review St. Ignatius' three situations of discernment and his classic interpretation of the meaning of consolation and desolation.
- Consider also the group's need to take as a prayerful discernment concern the discernment issue in question.
- Don't overlook "Revelation Time" in relation to the matter before you.
- Devote some time now to decision making as described in Situation Three and try to come to consensus on a decision

needing prayer. If time is too limited, continue the discussion in various settings throughout the church after the retreat.
- Persevere until you have a decision to pray about in what St. Ignatius called Situation Two—"Discernment Time."
- After devoting forty-five minutes to the procedure, discuss this experience. Name the learnings, benefits, and challenges found in this approach. *Try to arrive at specific recommendations on ways your church can use this method.*

DECISION AND DISCERNMENT, PART TWO

Ask a previously selected person to review the Quaker Committee of Clearness described in paragraphs 22ff. on pages 45f.

Discuss ways to introduce this method of discernment into the everyday life of your congregation. For example:
- The pastor may mention in a sermon the concept of a Committee on Clearness, and encourage its use as a means of offering spiritual guidance to each other.
- Make copies of the description of the Committee of Clearness and distribute them to your group(s), or to your congregation as a whole, to encourage use of the method.
- You may call for volunteers who want to form a Committee of Clearness and allow time during this retreat to begin the process of selecting the committee.
- Invite two volunteers to role-play a request that one serve on a Committee of Clearness.
- In groups of four or five, talk about times in the church when this practice could have been helpful.

"I WOULD LIKE TO NOMINATE"

- Ask the person assigned (preferably the chair of the nominating committee) to discuss the role of the committee on nominations in a church seeking to develop spiritual discernment (see paragraphs 16–19 on pages 119–20).
- Reflect upon ideas that were presented. The group can only begin at the retreat to consider this important matter. For about a half-hour after the silence, prayerfully discuss any of the following points:
  - The statement that "what cannot be done in the Spirit of love should be left undone"
  - Nominations not made in a discernment mode

- Nominations conditioned by the goal of operating a church governed by spiritual discernment
- The nominating committee as the most important committee in the church
- The implications of the nominating committee meeting for a few times toward the end of the year, rather than meeting regularly as a prayer/discernment/nominating committee

What does this retreat group want to say to the nominating committee about the importance of their work and their methods of doing it?

- Invite groups of four or five to name persons in the church who are noted for their "ministry of care" or as persons whose spirituality commends them as leaders.
- Write the names on the board and find a way to celebrate the gift of having them as part of the congregation.

TWO TYPES OF CHURCHES

- Ask the discussion leader of "Two Types of Churches" to present a summary from the workbook.
- Ask whether the business-as-usual description typifies your church's decisions. Call for examples. (The leader should have some to suggest as reminders, but give people time to think of other instances of how the adversarial approach has had a negative effect.)
- Look again at ways the church committed to spiritual discernment makes decisions. Discuss which type of church the group would rather be in and why. Review the five steps described in paragraphs 13–15 on pages 118–19, and consider that model as a way for your church's groups to operate.

What changes need to be made? How shall the group begin? When? Be specific in the recommendations. You may wish to ask a group of three or four to meet during a break to write the recommendations that have been mentioned, and present them to the rest of the group before the retreat ends.

BEFORE YOU CLOSE

- Since many principles of spiritual discernment by consensus presented in the workbook could not be covered in the retreat, ask the group to skim through the workbook and to list additional items they want leaders to consider. As time permits, incorporate some of these suggestions into the retreat.

• In silence prepare for the following important step:
• Review the retreat and select significant lessons, procedures, changes, or recommendations that the group wishes to make. Convey these to the Follow-up Committee.

The Follow-up Committee is to call the church to accountability for fair consideration and implementation, where possible, of recommendations from retreat participants.

CLOSING: (Allow about forty-five minutes)

• Sing happy songs suitable for the occasion.
• Invite participants to show and describe the symbols they sculpted during the retreat. Also discuss the value of providing creative aids at other church meetings.
• Call for voluntary sharing of what the retreat has meant, important lessons, and any hopes people hold for your congregation to become a church that makes decisions through spiritual discernment.
• Ask the pastor to close with a five-minute homily during the Service of Holy Communion. (See #118 in *The Upper Room Worshipbook*.)

END OF THE RETREAT

*   *   *

AN AFTERWORD

As you discussed during the group meeting following Week Eight, the big question is now what?

After this beginning, you will eventually discover the full answer to that important question. Part of the answer is to put into practice what you have decided during this retreat.

But don't forget that only a few members of your church will have studied the workbook or attended the retreat. As you return to your church, be gentle, loving, and patient as you share your enthusiasm about the present and future of your church. The others will catch your positive spirit and, in time, they'll share your dream of a higher way to be the church. Remember that they want the same thing you want—a spiritually vital and alive church.

Begin wherever you can to share the rationale for, and the practices of, a church committed to developing spiritual discernment. Invite others to experience one small change at a time.